Voices of Michigan,
an Anthology of Michigan Authors

Volume III
2001

~~~~~

Foreword by Thomas Lynch,
a Michigan author and
Great Lakes Award Winner in the general
books category for the year 2000.

Voices of Michigan,
an Anthology of Michigan Authors
MackinacJane's Publishing Company
Box 475
Mackinac Island, Michigan 49757

i

Voices of Michigan,
an Anthology of Michigan Authors
Volume III

copyright©2001
First printing May, 2001

Published by
MackinacJane's Publishing Company
Box 475
Mackinac Island, Michigan

ISBN: 0-9667363-3-8
Library of Congress number 2001116632

Printed in the United States of America

Cover painting – Mary Hramiec-Hoffman
Pen and Ink sketches – Charlene A. Oestman
Cover Design – Robert Roebuck
Typesetter and Typist – Felecia Sharpe
Editor – Christina Dembek
Assistant Editor – Sharon Frost

Foreword

A hundred years ago, Constantine Cavafy wrote, in his poem "Voices":

> *Ideal and beloved voices*
> *Of those who are dead, or of those*
> *Who are lost to us like the dead.*
>
> *Sometimes they speak to us in our dreams;*
> *Sometimes in thought the mind hears them.*
>
> *And with their sound for a moment return*
> *Other sounds from the first poetry of our life –*
> *Like distant music that dies off in the night.*

The great Greek poet understood that we are haunted not only by language, but by voices too; not by the meaning of words alone, but by their acoustics as well. As with music, we may or may not "get" the sense, but if we listen closely, we will "get" the sound. Before it was a written and read thing, literature was a heard and a said thing – great stories, great poems, the news of the world, all were spoken aloud around home fires, hunting camps, and market stalls. Only later was it written down, published, sent out to the world at large as epic and scripture and newsprint.

The conversation between readers and writers is intimate, one-to-one. Writers are readers who come to the point where they have something of their own to add to the talk -- another turn in the story, a new character, another line, or another way of thinking about lines entirely. To write requires, the belief that when you sit down to it, you are keeping up your end of the conversation, that your voice is worthy; you belong at the table, by the fire, in the forum – wherever voices are raised.

The "voice" that writers are always pursuing is the one that survives the ordinary din of daily life, thrives on the voices most admired from the past, and emerges as the one and only voice that sounds like one's self speaking to one's self. The effort to say what is memorable and meaningful in one's own way is at the center of the writerly life. Having listened to the "ideal and beloved voices," the working poet, essayist, or fictionist first tries to hum the tune, then sing along, then go solo. Confronted with this life's unspeakable beauties, unspeakable pains, unspeakable wonders, unspeakable loves, the writer casts words into the void to make some sense out of the lives we lead. "Let me say this about that" is the motivation. "Is anyone out there listening?" is the wonderment.

The writers in this collection are no exception. They proffer work done in private for public consideration. Their publication in this volume speaks to their eagerness to get their fictions and poems and non-fictions not only told, but heard – to get their singular versions on the record, to put the sound of the voice they speak to themselves in, into the ears of perfect strangers.

The chance that writers take, of course, is that their words will not haunt, their voices will not last, the sounds will not, in the end, make sense. It is that fear that keeps most writers silent. The chance that every reader takes, opening a collection like the one you hold, is that they will. Something you encounter here may "with their sound for a moment return/ other sounds from the first poetry of our life." Voices that align perfectly with our own amplify our lives in ways that change us forever. They come to us in dreams; they inhabit our thinking. When we find ourselves lost for words – in the face of great hope, great love, great hurt, great events -- these voices return to us. They are, as Cavafy knew, words made flesh. The *first poetry of our life – like distant music that dies off in the night* is the heart's iambic code, our own voice speaking to our self, and writing that gets to that pure center of creation outlives its maker. It becomes part of the lasting and

Voices of Michigan

larger chorus of *ideal and beloved voices*. The making of a book that gathers new stories, new poems, and new essays is a risky transaction, a brave enterprise, and an honorable one. Something here might outlive its maker. Something here might haunt. Something here might sound like the first poetry of our life. The voices assembled in **Voices of Michigan** present themselves to you. I am honored to introduce them.

Thomas Lynch
Milford, Michigan

Thomas Lynch is the author of three collections of poems and two collections of essays. He is a life-long resident of Michigan.

Contest Information

Voices of Michigan, an Anthology of Michigan Authors, is the product of a statewide refereed writing contest. Michigan writers are urged to submit poems, short stories or works of non-fiction to the contest. A panel of judges reads each of the entries, and determines which are to be included in the anthology.

The entries need not be about Michigan, and the writer need not live in Michigan. For more in-depth information on the contest, one can visit the **Voices** website: **www.voicesofmi.com**, contact the publishers via email at **macjanes@juno.com**, write the publishers at **Voices of Michigan,** Box 475, Mackinac Island, Michigan 49757 or call the publishers at 478.953.5995 or 906-478-3802. The entry deadline for Volume IV--which will be published spring 2002--is August 1, 2001.

Acknowledgement

Clearly Michiganders enjoy writing and more importantly enjoy seeing their words in print. Being one of the vehicles that allows these emerging authors' dreams to come true is what gives us, the publishers, of the anthology so much pleasure. And the other reward comes from how well-received *Voices of Michigan, an Anthology of Michigan Authors* has been throughout the state!

Three area businesses are sponsoring the book signing party June 17, 2001 at the Island House Hotel on Mackinac Island, Michigan, and they are: **Dale Hull** of the **Crooked Tree Arts Center** located in Petoskey**, Judith Mabee** from **Harbor Wear** with stores located in Petoskey and Harbor Springs, and **Al** and **Sharon Frost** from **Frost Lakefront Log Homes** which operates out of Petoskey**.** Thanks for your public support of our writing project.

The biggest round of applause goes to two young Petoskey friends. Without them there would be no **Voices** this year, and they are **Christina Dembek**, who among other volunteer efforts has served as our editor, and **Sharon Frost**, another major volunteer for the project, has served as our assistant editor.

Thanks to **Mary Hramiec-Hoffman** for granting us permission to use her oil painting for our cover. The painting incorporates the Michigan state wild flower and tree, the Iris and the White Pine. Additionally, we feel fortunate to have discovered **Charlene A. Oestman** who graciously allowed us to use three of her sketches in the book and for the bookmark. **Robert Roebuck**'s skills as a graphic artist allow us to have a lovely cover for volume three. A huge thanks to **Felecia Sharpe**, the administrative secretary for the English Department at Fort Valley State University, for the many hours she spent at the keyboard typing and formatting the manuscripts.

Without our readers to judge the contest, we would be nowhere, so a public thank you to: **Joy Brown, Pam Meier,**

Suzanne Davis, Julie Chamberlain Foust, Patricia Cameron Cortright, Gary Cusack, Frederic Sibley, Nancy Martin, Cathy Kemp, Joan Maril, Ellen Spearel, Janet Rathke, Wini-Rider Young, Sharon Nelson Bown, David Maril, William R. McTaggart and Raenette Palmer.

~~Jane and John Winston

Contents

Non-Fiction:

Poetry:

Appendix:

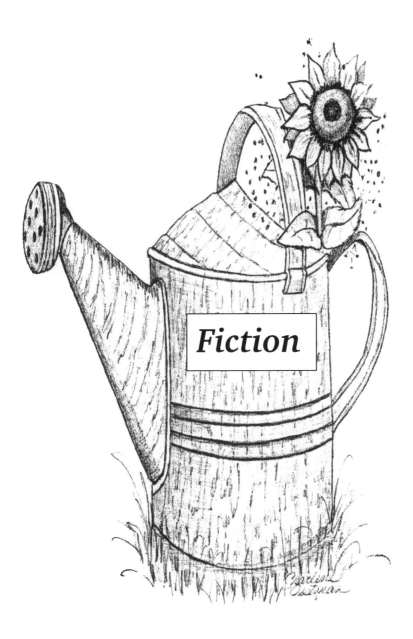

Fiction

Voices of Michigan

The Assassins

Gregory G. Barton

I know who killed John F. Kennedy. You can embrace the conspiracy theories, if you wish. Cling fast to Castro and his band of not-so-merry men. Hold the CIA close to your quivering heart. Keep one eye open for Russians, the Mafia, the second gunman, or even the mysterious man with the umbrella, if it'll help you sleep a little more soundly. But I was there. I saw him pull the trigger. I know who did it.

It was Corky.

I was eight years old when my family made its annual pilgrimage to Florida in the fall of 1963. My younger brother and I endured the long trek from Michigan while lying prone in the rear of our old station wagon. Dad folded down the back seat and tossed in a pile of blankets, while mom filled the remaining void with toys, food, comic books, and any other tranquilizing materials that she could lay her hands on. Lord knows what they were thinking. Granted, this was long before the days of mandatory seat belts, but it didn't take a physics degree to realize what would have happened to us in the event of an accident --launched through the windshield like a pair of missiles clad in cut-offs and matching Beanie and Cecil T-shirts.

We entered Miami Beach the same way we always did, from the north end of its magical strip, which allowed for a ceremonial procession past those fabled icons of tourism: *The Shellborne, The Fountaine Bleu, The Desert Inn, The Surfcomber, The Dunes, The Castaways*; each with its own aura, its own distinct gaudiness, its own devoted clientele. Our loyalty belonged to a motel called *The*

Gregory G. Barton is a writer and residential architect who grew up outside of Detroit, in Livonia. His collection of fictional golf stories entitled "On the Fringe" is due in bookstores this summer. Gregory currently resides with his wife and two sons in Lafayette, California.

Aztec, a rambling stucco beast that squatted close to the water's edge. Apparently, the brutal laws of nature also had applications in the world of hostelry, for each year we returned to find that the beast had extended its lair by devouring one of its weaker neighbors. We'd also find Corky waiting for us.

He was a year or two older than me, red headed and freckled, and already well down the long, slippery road to obesity. He came to Miami each year with a mother unfortunate enough to find herself divorced in a time when it wasn't nearly so chic. She would lie by the pool all day long striving for the tan that never surfaced. Always in the same white straw hat and frumpy bathing suit, always with a Coppertone stained paperback lying open across her stomach, always alone--politely yet firmly shunned by the wholesomeness of the American family.

That was also the year an outsider managed to infiltrate our little circle, a dark-haired boy about my brother's age, with a toothy grin and a startling square face. Corky instantly dubbed him Blockhead, so quickly; in fact, that I don't think I ever did learn his real name. Together, the four of us lived those precious few days with an intensity known only to children who would otherwise be mired in a snowbound classroom with nothing but close gray skies and a falling barometer waiting just the other side of the final bell. It was like a stay of execution, and we were determined to wring the sweet nectar of our fleeting childhood from every last moment.

Each morning we rose early and raced to the sea, not to beat the beachcombers to the conch shells and other precious flotsam, but to run and jump on the shimmering, oily--blue man-o-war jellyfish that had washed ashore the previous night, delighting at the satisfying pop their bubble-like bodies made beneath our tennis shoes. We would sit for hours at the feet of the mystical "Hat Man" as he wove his palm-leaf creations and tales of scorpion encounters with equal dexterity. The limbo dancers mesmerized us as they slithered ever lower beneath their golden bar, and then lower still, until their bronzed shoulders kissed the hot sand. Whole days were devoted to catching the chameleons that

4

haunted the alien shrubbery, releasing the poor creatures only after pulling off their tails so we could watch them writhe and twitch long after the rest of the lizard had disappeared. Great forts of sand were defiantly built just beyond the surf line, inviting desperate battles against the tide--which were lost--forcing us to fall back and dig into new positions that were just as quickly besieged and overrun by the sea's endless strategy of advance... retreat... advance... retreat.

If all else failed, one of our parents could always be found and systematically tormented. My father was a favorite target. We'd wait until he fell asleep on the beach, then sneak up and fill his oddly hollow chest with sand. One day he woke to this indignity, rose up on his elbow and said, "Why don't you boys wade out a couple of feet into the water and get lost in the Bermuda Triangle?"

"What's that, Daddy?" my brother asked.

"It's a place where weird things happen," he said before turning over. It was a brilliant move on his part (I can imagine him smiling into his towel even now), because we spent the entire afternoon roaming the surf in a vain quest for the supernatural.

The next day it rained. By mid-morning we were desperate enough to shuffle into the formerly scorned craft room run by a middle-aged woman known as Miss Sandy. She gave us idiotic plaster figurines that we glumly painted with idiotic colors. Just after lunch, the sky really let go, sending curtains of water that we tried to visually part for signs of a break in the storm. We loitered together on the brink of panic when it became obvious that none was coming.

"What do you want to do, Corky?" I asked as we sat in the lobby, swinging our feet off the end of a vinyl couch.

"Heck if I know," he said, shoving a handful of M&M's into his mouth. "There's nothing *to* do."

"But we're on vacation," my little brother pleaded, very close to tears. "There *has* to be something to do!"

5

"Well there ain't, so shut up," snapped Corky, whipping a red M&M across the tiled floor. We watched in silence as a man came out of the rest room and crushed it under his flip-flops.

"I know," ventured Blockhead, "let's play assassinate the president."

It was one of those rare moments of inspired genius. Assassinate the president! My brother and I sat in mute wonder of the possibilities, and Corky–who I knew thought of Blockhead in literal terms–grinned broadly, and wrapped a beefy arm around the smaller boy's neck.

We split up into two teams, each armed with water pistols purchased from the motel gift shop. The younger boys acted as the president and his faithful bodyguard, while Corky and I garnered the plum roles of the dreaded assassins. We gave them a fifteen-minute head start before giving chase.

The pursuit led from the steaming machinery and snaking pipes of the basement, to treacherous rooftops slick with rain and guano left behind by the generations of seagulls that roosted along the parapets. We dangled from slippery fire escapes, hid inside the huge commercial washers and dryers, careened into guests along the narrow corridors, monopolized the elevator, and screamed past a sulking crowd of grownups as they huddled around the cabana bar while clinging tightly to their cocktails.

Time and again we caught a glimpse of our quarry: a couple of heads hovering above a cascading pile of unused lounge chair cushions; two small bodies streaking along an upper balcony; a pair of feet disappearing around the corner at the far end of a long hallway. Each encounter was closer than the one before, and our excitement grew as the gap diminished. Twice we thought we had them cornered, only to let them slip through our fingers. But in the end something as simple as a wrong turn trapped the prey in the second-floor game room. Corky pressed his wide back against the doorjamb and leaned into the opening. A stream of water shot over his head and splattered against the opposite wall.

"Cover me!" he gasped, diving through the doorway and behind the pop machine, while I wildly sprayed the far end of the room. He returned the favor with a withering volley as I belly flopped my way beneath a row of pinball machines. Slowly, we advanced, inch by inch, game by game, driving them back, popping up just long enough to draw their precious liquid fire, which sheeted off the game tops and dripped onto the small of my back. By the time we had reached the last pair of pinball machines, the return fire had ceased altogether. Someone cursed from the corner of the room, and a bright yellow water gun bounced off the Skeeball game next to Corky and skittered across the floor.

My brother rose from behind the chalk-scarred pool table and, with a valiant yell of defiance, emptied the last of his water in my direction. I ducked behind the table, rolled to my left, and brought my own weapon to bear.

Blockhead dove in front of my brother and cried, "You can't shoot! He's the president!"

I pulled the trigger and a wet stain spread rapidly across the Secret Service man's chest. Corky then took careful aim and sent a lethal stream straight between my brother's brown eyes.

Nothing happened for a full minute, we all just stood there staring at each other as the water dripped off the end of my brother's nose. Then Corky let out a loud whoop and we all dutifully followed suit.

"Wow!"

"Cool!"

"Let's do it again!"

Arm in arm in arm in arm, like the gang from the Wizard of Oz, the four of us skipped down the main lobby's spiral staircase. Before we were halfway down, we knew something was wrong. Knots of people stood here and there in obvious distress and confusion, while the bellboys huddled near the front desk and conversed in reverent whispers. One couple sat on a bright orange couch sobbing uncontrollably, their children and luggage strewn about their feet.

A weeping Miss Sandy stumbled by us with her make-up in streaks.

"What is it, Miss Sandy?" Corky asked. "What's the matter?"

"Didn't you boys hear the announcement over the loud speaker?" she asked with a puzzled expression.

"No. What announcement?"

"Oh, it's just awful, Cork," she answered, wiping her cheeks with a flowered tissue. "Some damn fool's gone and shot Jack Kennedy."

Of all the memories I carry from that day, one stands out in sharper focus from the rest. It's the image of the man who stood alone in the middle of the lobby, silhouetted against a huge plate glass window that looked over the ocean. He stood very still, with his back to me, staring out at the rain, and from my vantage point it appeared he was about to embark down the path that meandered between two rows of palm trees as they marched down to the sea. An enormous, overstuffed suitcase hung from each arm, and, although they must have weighed a hundred pounds each, he chose to hold them as he stood there, rather than let them fall to the floor. From the set of his shoulders I knew that he would always carry that burden.

The Warren Commission scared the crap out of us, and we lived constantly in fear of men with dark suits and sunglasses who might swoop down like birds of prey and carry us off into oblivion. Each night in the months that followed, my brother, flashlight in hand, made his way down the narrow hall that led to the my bedroom sanctuary. Beneath the covers we tried to confront the mystery.

"How could it be?" we would ask the darkness. "How could four dumb kids kill the President of the United States a thousand miles away?" For there was never any doubt in our young minds that we were in some way responsible--that we were *involved*. We had never played that game before and we would never play it again. Did that make it pure coincidence, or just one of those odd anomalies that occur in every child's life–the kind that make us question our memory as we gaze back from the impossible distance of adulthood?

It was my brother who eventually offered the explanation that we came to embrace.

"Maybe Dad had it all wrong," he said one night as the glow from his upturned Eveready garishly lit the underside of his chin and highlighted his nostrils. "Maybe the Bermuda Triangle doesn't stop at the beach; maybe part of it sticks into the game room."

It was not long afterward that he stopped climbing into bed with me.

As for Corky, he and his mother left for New York the morning after that terrible day and never came back. Sometimes, when the weather turns particularly wet, I'll let my thoughts fall on the memories of my old friend, wondering how far his road has taken him. I don't know if they'll catch him or not; I just hope he doesn't squeal on us if they ever do.

Voices of Michigan

Kisses For Laura

Joan Roth

The cold, windy corner is deserted, except for a rumpled scarecrow not exactly a scarecrow, just me, skinny Laura Grey. Frizzy, dishwasher hair, pointy nose, and arms and legs like four bent sticks. I'm twelve years old and I'm freezing to death.

And if the bus doesn't come by the time I count to one hundred, I'm going home.

It's a lie. I'm not going home. I'm going to the City Library. On Sunday afternoons that's what I do. I sit by the radiator and read until closing time at five o'clock.

I'd take books home with me but I can't unless I have a library card, which I don't, and I can't get one unless I live in the city, which I don't.

We used to live in the city. Before my father lost his job. He didn't lose it exactly, like you lose a handkerchief, but he lost it just the same or he wouldn't be out looking for it all the time. My mother cleans houses, other people's, not ours. We don't have any money. Nobody has any money, for goodness sake; it's 1935. Do I sound grouchy?

It's that awful Christmas party at school. On Friday we drew names for gifts. I drew Rosemary's name! The most popular girl in sixth grade, and the nicest. I can't even hate her.

And I'm freezing because the bus won't come. Wouldn't you be grouchy?

> Following retirement from the University of Michigan, **Joan Roth (Schmeichel)** moved up North with her husband where their five children and fourteen grandchildren visit. Her writing includes curriculum materials in reading workbooks for second through eighth grade. Joan envisions *Kisses for Laura* as the first in a series featuring her character.

The bus must have heard me because it puffs down the road. I drop my pennies in the box and sit behind the driver. That's where the heat is.

. . . . .

I finish **Anne of Green Gables** just as the library's closing bell sounds. Anne's picture shows she's a bit skinny. Maybe skinny's all right. Maybe skinny's better than Mrs. Praeter, my teacher, who's round and gray like a pigeon.

I shove my skirt back in my snowpants. My mother says it's to invite pneumonia to let the wind blow up your skirts. I don't think you invite pneumonia. I think it just comes. But if it blows up your skirts, every girl in my class would have it.

I tuck my skirt in because my mother gets after me enough, usually over my grades. Mrs. Praeter says my mind wanders. It doesn't really go places, like to Africa, it just doesn't pay attention.

I pull on my old socks for mittens and tiptoe down the stairs. One time when I was leaving, my bus money dropped through a hole in my pocket. It clanged on each step. The librarian pointed to the "**silence**" sign on her desk. This time I make it safely out the door.

My bus waits on the corner, gray smoke blowing out its tail.

It's a windy ten miles home with the bus rocking and bucking across the road. I hang on to my seat until I see the lights of Zancowski's grocery store. This is where I get off, at Oakwood Subdivision.

Oakwood sits in open fields in one of the coldest states in the forty-eight. My mother says a job and indoor plumbing are everything in Oakwood. I wouldn't know. We don't have either.

It's pitch dark in Oakwood except for tiny specks of light marking some of the houses. I'm anxious to see if ours is one of them. Light means somebody's home and a fire burns in the black iron stove.

Most days I build the fire. A layer of paper, a layer of coal, a few drops of kerosene from the red can outside the kitchen door, a match, then slam the door.

Fire is terrible in the country. Often at night I hear sirens calling out the volunteers and know somebody's outside in the snow.

Tonight, everybody, even my mother, is home for dinner. Everybody's Edward, who's eighteen, tall, thin, serious, and a senior in high school. Thomas is fifteen, wears a big grin, is not serious, and wants to quit ninth grade three days out of five. Elizabeth is sixteen, in eleventh grade, has blazing red hair, and a temper to match.

Edward and Thomas help Gimpy McGee, who lives by the creek, deliver packaged coal and cans of kerosene to the neighborhood. Elizabeth takes care of the Wadkin's kids after school. Sometimes I sit for Violet Willie whose brain isn't as big as she is, her mother says.

Everybody in my family loves to talk, except me. I love to listen. Thomas starts with Old Mrs. Lockgaar, one of Gimp's customers. She keeps chickens that fly the coop all the time. Thomas chases after them. He calls it round-up time.

Old Mrs. Lockgaar sends feathers over for our beds and a chicken now and again. I see her outside every morning on my way to school.

This morning is no exception. You'd think she'd stay inside where it's warm. Today is especially bad, too. The snow squeaks underfoot and cold glues the insides of your nose together.

A creek wanders through our fields. It winds up by the school. Its high banks block the wind so I usually drop inside and slide on the ice.

Red Ridge School, as it's called for no reason, is about a mile from our house. It looks like a brick shoebox. Everybody from kindergarten through twelfth grade goes there.

My sixth grade classroom is down the hall on the first floor. A coat rack stands outside the door for jackets and lunches. My lunch is in a clean, white bag today. Once I had to use an onion sack. I keep a sharp eye out for good bags now.

Mrs. Praetor hasn't arrived yet. You can tell by the noise inside the classroom. When I open the door, everybody stops, and then starts up again.

Sixth grade is a square room with windows on one side and Mrs. Praetor's desk and blackboard up front. Rows of wood and metal desks run up and down the middle. They're screwed to the floor so they don't get moved by accident. A bookcase stands against the back wall and a Christmas tree is right beside it. Paper chains and snowflakes decorate the tree. Christmas always brightens the room.

Rosemary waves to me. She waves to everybody. Didn't I tell you she was nice? I wave back before heading to my seat. The room buzzes with talk. Except for Florence Cox, who doesn't talk to anybody. She sits hunched over by the window. Every day she stares outside.

I guess if there's one person in the whole world worse off than I am, it's Florence. She has lank hair that lets both ears peek out and a whispery voice so low that nobody can hear what she says even if they wanted to which they don't.

Florence lives in an old house by the school. It used to have a porch but doesn't any more, just some broken boards hanging loose. Florence has younger brothers and sisters. Her mother screams at them every recess and lunch hour.

I feel sorry for Florence and sometimes want to talk to her. I don't try very hard though and feel guilty about it.

Why are some girls so lucky? Rosemary, for example, has everything and Florence, nothing. I guess I have almost nothing.

Mrs. Praetor comes in and announces an arithmetic drill. I hate drills. I'm the last one standing and the first one sitting. I can't think on my feet. As soon as I stand up, my brains sink to my toes.

The morning passes slowly as I wait for lunchtime. Finally, the bell rings and I take my new bag to my desk. Everybody eats at their desk, except for Florence and some others who go home. After lunch, we go outside. That's the rule.

"Fox and geese!"

"Fox and geese!"

Everybody wants to play the game where a "fox" chases a bunch of "geese" around a wagon wheel tramped out in the snow.

As I wander across the playground, hoping Rosemary will ask me to play, a voice yells at me. It's a voice that you know comes with red hair and freckles. Sheldon! Lately, every time I'm around, he throws snowballs or something. I hate it. He's big and clumsy and even dumber in school than I am.

"Duck, Leery!" he yells, calling me by that nickname that he made up out of nothing at all. "Here I come."

Before I can move, he's leap-fogging over my back, shoving me into the snow. I spit slush from my mouth and screech at him.

"Sheldon, you're a hoodlum!" my mother's favorite word, "A dim witted imbecile," Elizabeth's favorite, and "a snip nose!" my own. "I hate you!" For good measure, I add, "Someday I'm going to give you a smack!"

Everybody stops what they're doing. They stare. They shriek with laughter. Sheldon claps his hands and jumps up and down.

"Leery, Leery!" he calls, "Someday I'll give YOU a smack, like this." He puckers up.

My face burns. I swallow hard. What have I done? Rosemary comes up and pats my shoulder, to show she understands. But the laughter continues until, finally, the ringing bell lets me escape.

The rest of the day, every time the teacher's back is turned, one of the boys puckers up and points to Sheldon.

What if he tries to catch me? Can I outrun him? I wonder for the millionth time how I could have been so stupid. Everybody knows a smack is a kiss, for goodness sake.

The final bell rings and I jump up. I can be out the door before Sheldon moves. I can be halfway home before he gets his boots on.

I peek out the front door. No one's around. I sneak outside. Sheldon leaps from behind the school. He's followed by a cluster of rowdy boys.

"Pucker up, Leery."

"Cheeks like roses, nose like hoses."

I run as fast as I can. I know Sheldon's lumbering behind me. I can hear his laughter. I run half-way home before chancing a look. There's no one but Ellen Allen who's a year younger than I am and lives in the subdivision.

Ellen and I play together sometimes. Not too often, because she can't come to my house and I can't go to hers when her father's home. That's because Ellen's father hates my mother, since she called him a hoodlum and an animal when he cuffed his wife outside Zancowski's grocery store.

Ellen wants me to come over to play paper dolls. Usually we play 'most beautiful,' where Ellen gets to be the most beautiful girl in the world and I get to be what's left.

We follow a path that branches off from the creek to Ellen's back porch. It's hung with gray rags stiffening in the cold but her kitchen is warm and Mrs. Allen friendly.

She grins at us now from her post by the oil stove where she's keeping a cup of tea warm. Mrs. Allen's a tall, stooped woman with bare legs, bulging veins, and a missing tooth in front. None of this seems to bother her much. I like Mrs. Allen and guess I could sometimes be most beautiful if we were ever to play together.

I stay longer than I should. It's dark when I walk up the front path to our house. Ours is a tar-paper covered place about the size of the sixth grade classroom. Roses climb the walls in summer OK, but in winter the roses look like hair that needs combing. Like mine, I guess.

I pound on the door. An angry Thomas lets me in, demanding to know where I've been.

"Elizabeth and I have been hollering all over for you and Edward's on his way back to school."

This is serious. My brothers stick together since the Klewicki boys caught Thomas behind Gimpy's place and gave him a licking. Gimpy's orange-haired girlfriend chased them off. We didn't tell our mother, of course. She would have marched over and given the Klewickis a piece of her mind. We try to avoid that.

I promise to come straight home from school--and wash everybody's socks for a week. I guess it could have been worse. I forget about Sheldon.

In the morning, I'm so preoccupied, I reach school without noticing the cold. The first word I hear is smack. I want to smack somebody.

All week it's the same. Sheldon teases me and the other boys egg him on. I get used to it. I guess you can get used to anything. Still, I run home most days.

Before I know it, it's Thursday and the Christmas party is the very next day. I've tried not to think of the party, of Rosemary's gift.

"I'll have to tell her what it is," I announce to Edward who is doing his homework at the table. "She'll never in a million years know if I don't tell her."

I have to admit that the blue satin handkerchief case cut from my mother's old slip is beautiful. I sewed on pink ribbons and embroidered pink flowers in the corners.

"I'll still have to tell her what it is." I apply a Santa Claus sticker to the wrapped package.

"Are you talking to me?" Edward asks after I'm finished and half way up the ladder to the attic.

"No, I was talking to Santa Claus."

"Oh." He goes back to work.

Edward's like that sometimes. It never bothers me. I have other things to think about, like my clothes.

I wrap myself in the quilt on the bed that I share with Elizabeth and think about self-improvement. My hair is the worst. Maybe I can roll it up like Elizabeth. Maybe I can pull it back. Maybe I can shave it off.

Forget the hair. Maybe I can borrow Elizabeth's skirt. If I roll it at the waist and borrow one of her sweaters to hide the roll? Elizabeth's navy sweater is perfect, except for a hole in the sleeve. I can mend that.

"Elizabeth," I call when she comes in.

Extracting vows of cleanliness and obedience, she loans me her clothes. I mend the sweater with white thread, all that I can find, and dab a little ink on it.

After dinner I climb back to the attic. It's a cozy place, filled with bright feather beds and quilts. All it needs is heat. I snuggle down. Only two days before Sunday. Maybe I can find another book like **Anne of Green Gables**.

Friday morning I open my eyes to a soft white blanket on the bed, a dusting of snow that came in through the cracks in the wall.

"I could be buried until spring," I call to Elizabeth who is already up and dressed.

"Just be sure to shake the quilts when you get up," she tells me.

Elizabeth never seems to get cold. Maybe she stays warm because of her red hair. I blush, thinking about Sheldon's red hair.

If I stay in bed, I'll miss the party. But my mother would find out. I get up and dress in Elizabeth's clothes. The skirt hangs on my bones. I want to cry but the tears will freeze on my face before they change the skirt. I slip into a rumpled dress and cover it with Elizabeth's sweater.

When I climb downstairs, everyone is gone, but oatmeal and stewed prunes wait for me. I gulp everything down before leaving.

As I walk by Old Mrs. Lockgaar's, she beckons me over. Today she's wrapped in dead Old Mr. Lockgaar's giant sweater. Both pockets bulge.

She begins by saying as she heard how I liked to read and how she could never see much sense in it herself and I was welcome to these if I wanted them. She finishes with a little cackle and pulls two thick books from her pockets.

I'm so surprised by the length of the speech--I had never heard Old Mrs. Lockgaar say more than half a dozen words--that it takes a minute to realize what I hold in my hands.

Two books by Charles Dickens! I can hardly believe my eyes. I surprise Old Mrs. Lockgaar, and myself, with a yell so loud that the old woman claims her chickens won't lay for a month. She pokes me with a bony finger and tells me to leave the books and pick them up after school, that I better get going.

I take her advice and don't think once of Rosemary's present or Sheldon's smacks.

Everything and everybody in school sparkles today. The students are dressed in Sunday bests. The boys wear corduroy knickers and sleeveless sweaters. They sport clean fingernails and slicked-back hair. The girls are fluffed in dresses and party jumpers.

When I see Rosemary, I gasp. She wears pink velvet with big puffy sleeves and a wide ribbon at the waist. Her blond hair, tied with pink ribbons, hangs in giant sausages, only much prettier of course.

Everybody crowds around her, everybody except Florence, that is, who sits in her usual seat, wearing her usual brown jumper and dirty white blouse. I'm glad I have Elizabeth's sweater on. I can't hope to look like Rosemary but I feel like a better Laura.

I slide my gift under the tree and take my seat. Nobody teases me, not one person. I glance at Sheldon. He's busy slicking down his hair with one big freckled hand and examining the cracked plaster on the ceiling while whistling "Deck the Halls."

He looks sillier than usual, in a green sleeveless sweater that must have belonged to his father from the way it hangs on him. I turn away and roll my own sleeves up until they just touch the wrist bone.

The day drags on. I'm not looking forward to the party, for goodness sake, but want to start my new books. Sheldon continues to ignore me and the "smack" seems forgotten. Everybody is too busy giggling and passing notes to think about me.

Finally, three o'clock arrives. Desks are cleared. Mrs. Praeter selects a few students to set up for the party. The rest may go to the lavatory.

I'm surprised to be chosen to help. It has never happened before. Mrs. Praeter asks me to distribute her gift to the students, a red paper Christmas stocking with a striped candy cane inside. While I do this, she brings in a steaming pot of hot cocoa.

In a minute, the rest of the class returns, excited and noisy:

"Quit shoving!"

"You'll muss my dress."

"Get off my shoes!"

Mrs. Praeter hushes everybody by writing "Silent Night" on the blackboard. She begins to sing "Deck the Halls," and we join in with gusto, especially the "fa, la, la" part. Next, Rosemary plays Santa Claus and passes out the gifts

Mrs. Praeter has the most gifts, with everybody trying to give her something. I made a pinecone snowman to hang on her tree. The next biggest pile is on Rosemary's desk. But everybody has at least one gift, plus Mrs. Praeter's stocking.

Mrs. Praeter fills our milk cups from her steaming pot, then says "Merry Christmas." That's the signal. Wrapping paper flies amidst squeals and shrieks, yells and whoops, and some groans.

I'm in dread, too nervous to open the brown paper package on my own desk. I watch Rosemary. She has my gift in her hands. She unties the string. I hold my breath. I squeeze down in my seat.

"How pretty," her voice comes across the room. "A handkerchief case. And I have a new handkerchief right here to put in it. Thank you, Laura."

Rosemary is looking right at me. I can hardly believe my ears! She knows what it is! She even likes it, unless she's just being nice. But it doesn't matter. She knows what it is. I don't have to tell her.

Now I can turn to my own gift. As I do, a small, fretful voice floats down from somewhere around my left ear. It's Florence and she's saying something too painful to speak aloud.

"Leery," she whispers. "Ain't but one piece gone n' yer so foxy, you kin fer certain make another." The voice stops a moment, then continues on before fading away altogether. "It's all I had."

I look at my Christmas gift. It's a used puzzle with, as Florence said, one piece missing. I feel a sharp stab of disappointment, and a sadness. Christmas is never as good as it's supposed to be. Then I remember Florence. Too late. She's already gone back to her seat.

I sort through my desk to find pencil and paper. "I hate stupid, boring puzzles," I write. "This one will be twice as hard and twice the fun." I start to sign it "Laura" but change my mind and write "Your friend, Laura." I pass the note over to Florence and watch her face brighten as she reads it.

The puzzle is the three Wise Men, now mostly only two. I blink and turn to my hot cocoa. Suddenly a thought comes to me. Foxy? Nobody has ever called me foxy before. I feel a smile building on my face. I look at the puzzle again and then carefully put the lid back on.

The party ends. We clear our desks of all signs of Christmas. I fill the brown paper bag I brought from home with Mrs. Praeter's Christmas stocking and my new puzzle.

In the hall I pull on snowpants and galoshes and don't complain once, not even when I see snow swirling outside the school door. I tuck my paper bag inside my coat and leave.

Cold air and wet flakes smack into my face. I'm glad my Christmas things are hidden away. Icy crystals settle on my eyelids and blur the road in front of me. I clutch the bag tight under my coat.

As I pass by Florence's house, I hear a voice whistling through the snow.

"Leery!"

"Leery, wait!"

My heart begins to thump. I want to run. I grit my teeth and duck my head to keep the snow out of my eyes. I watch the road where drifting snow is beginning to hide the ditch alongside.

Suddenly I feel a tug on my arm. Gentle as it is, I jump and begin to shake. A blurred face and frosted red hair shoves its way right in front of my nose. The "smack" is coming. I know it. I should have run, after all.

"Merry Christmas, Leery!" Sheldon's voice sounds hoarse. He pushes a small, white bag into my hand, then disappears into the next gust of snow.

I look fearfully at the bag. I hold it away from me. Is it a firecracker ready to go off? I shake it. Nothing happens. I turn my back to the wind. Shielding the bag from the snow, I look inside.

A dozen taffy candy kisses rest underneath a folded note. "Kisses for Laura," the note says.

My cheeks feel hot instead of cold, and my eyes are wet. I brush the snow off my coat and unbutton it. Sheldon's gift goes in the bag, right beside my puzzle from Florence and the Christmas stocking from Mrs. Praeter.

First, I'll go to Old Mrs. Lockgaar's. Then I'll go home and build a fire. Then I'll sit by the stove in the blue chair with my Christmas gifts around me.

I laugh and kick the snow into puffy clouds. They dance around my face and don't feel cold at all.

As Far As She Could Go

Lynn Helene Moody

The girl slept fitfully, red hair loose on the pillow like copper silk on snow. In dreams she tried to be free.

In dreams it was winter, and as the girl slipped under the barbed-wire fence, her powder-blue ski vest snagged. She stopped in a huff of frozen breath, dropping her neon-orange sledding saucer in the snow. A rusted barb of the fence was embedded in the right shoulder of her ski vest. The girl lifted the wire, gingerly, in her mittened fingers, pull, rip.

"Oh, crap," she said out loud. Unconsciously, she looked around to see if anyone was there in the night, listening. A swollen moon glared at her from the western sky—its face almost a smirk. "All right for you," she said, sneering back at the moon.

> **Lynn Helene Moody** is a writer, medical scientist and mother of three. She has traveled extensively, including a six-year stint as an English teacher in Japan. One of her poems, *Sifting Sands*, has been published in The University of Maryland's *Paper Tracks*. Lynn has written several short stories and is in the middle of her first novel. She lives in Elk Rapids with her husband and daughters.

The girl remembered her older sister—Lena had taught her the different phases of the moon; its waxings and wanings. Together, each gazing in turn through the length of a telescope, they had discovered some of the moon's landmarks: Valles Rheita, Montes Alpes, and Lena's favorite seas, Mare Serenitatis and Mare Tranquillitatis.

Lena had been sixteen when she'd left home, leaving the telescope still fixed on the spot in the sky where the moon had been at nine o'clock the night she escaped. The girl never saw her big sister again. Though she had received two dog-eared, stained postcards, one from New York City, and the other from

Hollywood, California. Both were unsigned, but at the bottom of each postcard Lena had written: "P.S. Remember what I said!"

The girl remembered. She'd remembered for years now, though at the time, Lena's harshly whispered words hadn't made much sense. "I'll come back for you," Lena had said before she'd climbed out of the bedroom window, "I'll get you out of here." Just before she'd disappeared over the windowsill, Lena had whispered between tears, "I'm sorry." The girl hadn't known at the time what it was all about. She had cried and asked her sister not to go. The girl had been eleven, a completely happy eleven, with her own bedroom full of stuffed animals, and trees to climb, and the horses to ride, and no worries; she hadn't understood. It wasn't until a few days later that the girl had realized why her sister had run away. A few days was all it took to understand why Lena had said through tears, "I'm sorry."

The girl got up now, slowly, and brushed the snow from her blue jeans. They were soaked through. She picked up the plastic sledding saucer, a Christmas gift from her father when she was eight. It was fast and weathered, with patches of neon-orange sloughed off by a tree root or some rocks she had skidded over. The snow crunched as she resumed her trek.

Once before she had made this journey, in broad daylight, six long months after it had started. This same sort of early thaw it was, too—the air wet with melting, heavy when you breathed it in. As the temperature dropped again, the snow stole back the moisture, reclaiming it in a crystalline matrix that made the hill slick and fast. The icy snow sent her roaring down the slope and far and away, past her father, past her mother, past herself. She had no longer existed. She had been free. But after hours of flying, when she realized that in the end she had to go home or freeze to death, she knew. She knew that Lena would never come back for her; she knew that nothing would take her away from here. She went home and put the saucer up in the loft of the garage, holding a sad and lonely ceremony. Old friend. She hadn't touched it again until tonight.

Back then she had avoided the part of the hill for which she was now bound. Now, she knew the exact slope that she needed— the one that faced the wall. As she walked, the icy snow held her feet down, catching them in her own footprints again and again, as if to stop her. Cold crystalline pieces crowded around her ankles and slipped down inside her boots. A few times she stopped to dig them out with uncovered fingers, the mitten she held between her teeth tasting of caked-on dirt and rotting yarn. She gave up, trudging on with ankles numb in defense against the biting cold.

She was crossing an open field belonging to the Howard's, a family of horse farmers. Stray clumps of old corn stalks poking up through the snow sagged in the moonlight. They were tired, too. The girl stopped. The snow gleamed in the light from the bloated moon, and the girl could see, as if it were daylight, the orchard ahead of her and the snow-covered slope of the hill like a bridal gown rising up behind the trees. For a few moments she was lifted. She could see the hill in the way it looked in summer with the green running all the way down to the orchard. She used to play there in innocence every day. Then, after, it had become her special ally, and she would hide there, reading her books, dreaming, and pretending she were somewhere else.

One late summer day she remembered vividly. She had galloped down the hill, pretending to ride Chesterfield, the Howard's black gelding. She had flung herself face-first into the deep soft grass that grew in the unkempt orchard. The smell of aging apples permeated the air, seeping into every inch of her, her hair, her skin. Eating the worm-holed apples along the way, she climbed the tallest tree. She clung to the top branch and dipped back and forth in the wind. She could see the acres of green and the deep blue of Lake Michigan beyond. The Howard's back paddock lay to the North, and the horses were running as she had, with their noses to the wind.

Chesterfield was the girl's favorite. She rode him whenever she got the chance, whenever Mrs. Howard would see her hanging on the corral fence and invite her to ride. Mrs.

Howard always said the girl looked so beautiful on Chesterfield with his deep black mane and tail—a perfect contrast to her hair, long and copper-red, flowing in the breeze. They would always ride together, Mrs. Howard taking Stormy, the gray mare.

Sometimes Mrs. Howard would pack a picnic for them. They would ride for hours, through the orchard, skirting around the base of the hill and on down to the lakeshore where they would stop at the old stone wall.

"This is just a piece of what used to be here. It was a huge fence that encircled the entire farmstead," Mrs. Howard had told her. "That was in the 1700's. There are a few piles of stones here and there, but this twenty-foot section is all that's still standing." Mrs. Howard spread out a patchwork quilt on the grass, and they feasted on freshly baked bread, cheese, sweet pickles that Mrs. Howard had canned, and dark chocolate brownies. "A few years ago, Mr. Howard nearly had a fit. There were some boys out here—the Parker boys—sledding down the hill straight at the wall. Daring each other to miss it. Playing chicken. Can you imagine? Mr. Howard was still fuming when he got back to the house and told me about it. I guess I've never seen him so mad—before or since."

The girl had tried to tell Mrs. Howard that day. Mrs. Howard didn't have children of her own, and the girl had dreamed that someday Mr. and Mrs. Howard would come to her rescue, snatching her away from her own weak, sobbing mother—taking her to live with them. In the end, she hadn't had the courage to tell Mrs. Howard. Now the girl had discovered that if she ever did tell, the State would come and get her and place her in foster care. The girl knew from friends at school that foster care was usually worse than anything else she currently endured.

Now, the rest of the cornfield lay between the girl and the orchard, and the orchard looked dark and cold. The girl was thirsty, so she laid the saucer on the snow and sat down on her knees on top of it. She scooped up some snow and put it in her mouth. It tasted like him. She spat it back, wiping her mouth severely. She sat for a moment, not wanting to cry, feeling lost in the field of white. Suddenly she scooped up huge handfuls of snow, cramming them into her mouth, spitting them back out. Hungrily, now, she shoved in more, rinsing and spitting. Other handfuls went to her face. She scrubbed. The girl thought that if she could just get clean, she could turn around. She wouldn't need the hill, or the saucer, or the wall. She could turn around and run as far as she could go and never come back—just like Lena. But the taste—the smell—never left her. It tainted everything. Slowly, she dropped her arms, chunks of ice still clutched in her hands. Her face was red and raw, and inside, her belly began to ache. She rose, grabbed the saucer, and slogged on.

When the girl reached the orchard she stopped, listening. A bitter wind played in the dry gnarled branches of the apple trees. The clacking and scraping sounded like the pairs of dead deer antlers that hung together in bunches in her father's butcher shop each November.

She had stolen one of his knives once, hiding it under her pillow. Each night she had practiced. First would come the shadow as he crossed the path of the hallway light that shone under her door. No sound to awaken her, just the shadow. She always saw it, though, as she lay there, waiting. The creaking of the door would start, low, then rise in pitch. In her plan, she would wait. She would wait for him to get started, then pull the knife from under the pillow, quietly, easily, and put it in the center of his back.

In the end she couldn't do it, and rather than risk returning the knife to the butcher shop, she had buried it here in the orchard, with a shock of her hair, under the lone pear tree.

For a moment, she thought she would go and look at the tree. Instead, she lowered her head and trudged on. The snow was deeper around the edge of the orchard. The saucer smacked against the back of her leg in a rhythm between steps—crunch, crunch, slap—until she reached the hill. The moon had begun to set in front of her now, egging her on. It threatened to slip behind the hill without her, and the girl took it as a challenge.

Without stopping, she climbed the slope in huge strides. She slipped once and steadied herself with the saucer. Only at the top did she pause. As she crested the top of the hill, the girl thought she saw a shadow move across the landscape, slowly, and then disappear.

The hill seemed expectant tonight; the slope was awash in a pink-orange glow, as if it had put on a pretty party dress for her. The moon, fat and burning, brooded over the blue-black lake, and a wide red path bled out from it, running along the smooth water, right up onto the snow, broken only by the old stone wall and its small shadow. This would make it easier. She could steer, using the moonlight, until it was blocked by the wall; by then, it wouldn't matter. She laughed at the moon, jumped on the saucer and went.

Air singed her cheeks, copper strands of her hair flapped in front of her eyes, and her heart fluttered like the wings of a dying bird. She felt again the soft feathers of the mockingbird she had found almost dead in the cornfield. The taste of the ripe apples from the orchard flooded her mouth. The wet, cold dirt from under the pear tree slipped through her fingers. She heard the muffled buzzing of the bees in Chesterfield's paddock on the days when the sun had covered her shoulders, and the clover's sweetness had filled her lungs. The wall was coming. She laughed again. She thought she might be going there now, back to the bees and the clover and the sunshine. The snow hissed. Gray stones, oddly shaped and stuck together with an ashen mortar—the wall was coming. As she closed her eyes, she thought of the sunlight and the clover and the horses in the pasture—she was riding Chesterfield again. This was it; she was free.

A bump. The saucer almost slipped out from under her. One leg came un-tucked, falling down. She was airborne—flying.

The girl woke up, bathed in sweat and moonlight. She looked around. The white lace curtains hung at her bedroom window. Moonlight pored in. Wasn't she free? Had she been here all along, asleep in her bed, waiting for him? Then the shadow came as the door was slowly pushed open, and she cowered down under her covers as far as she could go.

Voices of Michigan

Brotherly Love

M ary Lee Scott :)

Mary Lee Scott

Last week I had one of those major life-changing days, though I sure wouldn't have guessed that it was coming. It started out totally normal. My alarm woke me at 6:40 a.m., playing the Goo Goo Dolls. I like them—they have cool lyrics, not just the same old stuff about love all the time.

For just a second, I forgot. I forgot that my brother Luke was dead. I thought he was sleeping in the room next to mine, ready to wake up and fight with me over the Nintendo 64 or the last of the Lucky Charms.

And then I remembered. In an instant reality hit. I remembered the police

> **Mary Lee Scott** is an elementary school teacher. She lives in Galesburg, Michigan, with her husband and two sons, ages nine and twelve. She has written several short stories, one that was published in *Voices of Michigan*, Volume II. She is working on publishing her first novel.

at the front door, my parents crying, me going to my room and not coming out until I had cried by myself for a long time—and then I pushed it out of my mind. I'm getting better at this.

I got up, dressed, and went downstairs. Before going to the kitchen, I ran out back to see my dog. She's a yellow Labrador. Luke was never super crazy about Princess, but I adore her. She was dozing outside her doghouse in the fenced-in kennel, but leaped up, thumping her tail like crazy, when she saw me coming.

"Hi, girl," I said softly as she jumped up, trying to lick me. When we were little, she was always knocking us down, but I never minded. Luke used to cry, even though he was older and bigger. My dad says some people just aren't into animals, but he and I are. Princess walked me back to the house.

My mother was already up, making her lunch. My father had already gone to work. He has to leave at 6:00 A.M.

"Morning, Tom," said my mom. "How's it going?"

"OK, Mom," I said. "How's it going with you? Did you sleep?" My mother's been fighting insomnia since Luke died, although she doesn't like to talk about it. She looked even more tired than usual.

"Sure. I'm fine," she said too quickly, then turned to the refrigerator. "What do you want for breakfast?" She never seems to remember that I can fix my own meals, being fourteen years old. It's like she can't give it up or something. Luke used to give her grief about it, so I try not to.

"I'll just grab some cereal," I said.

"O.K." She sat down at the table with me, ready to begin some Quality Time. No matter how rushed, she always sits down with us when we eat. (She herself cannot eat before at least 10:00 A.M.) It used to seem odd to me, but now I really like it. Otherwise I'd be alone at the table, a concept I'm not ready to consider.

We chatted about our day and what we expected to happen. I had a history test and football practice; she had a staff meeting and a test to give (she's a fifth-grade teacher).

My dad called from work to say good morning. He's done that since I was a little kid; like the kitchen table, it now means more to me. "Good luck on the history test, Bud," he said to me. "Although I'm sure you'll do fine."

"Thanks, Dad. See you tonight. Be careful," I added before I hung up. I always say that; so does my mom. It's funny, because with him being a cop, I always figured he'd be the one to get injured. I worried about it all the time as a kid. I had nightmares about it sometimes.

Since Luke died, I don't dream much, and I never allow myself to think about anything happening to my parents. I'm not a very religious person, but I don't think God would do that to me.

I fed Princess and loaded my backpack, and by 7:30 A.M., my mom and I were packed and ready to go, me to the bus stop, her to school. I dreaded this. We stared at each other a minute, then she hugged me. There were tears in her eyes. The thing is, the last time she saw Luke was just before we got on the school bus, one day last spring.

"Have a great day," she said, as she has said every day since I started kindergarten. Of course, very few days ever truly qualify as great, but she keeps hoping.

"You, too, Mom," I said. I tried smiling at her, but it felt like I was making a face, pulling my lips back and baring my teeth like a wild animal. "I'll see you after football. Pick me up at 5:00?" I tried to keep it light, like things were normal, the way they used to be.

"OK, I'll see you then," she said quickly, then we headed out. She drove off without waving because Luke had told her years ago that she was embarrassing us to death. She said of course, she understood, and that we should tell her any time we felt uncomfortable.

Luke got a big kick out of this. Dad finally had to tell him to stop making her feel bad, and to be grateful for such a loving mother. I agreed with Dad on this one. I didn't think she went overboard. I also recall Luke being the one who hugged her longest at bedtime.

On the bus, I saw my best friend Jimmy. He has been a huge help to me these last few months. I get him to come over for dinner as often as I can, because he sits in Luke's chair. Dinner with just me and my folks is the absolute worst, because we all go out of our way not to mention Luke, or to look in the direction of his chair. Everybody's polite and cheery, and careful.

"What's up, Tom?" said Jimmy.

"Not much," I replied, dropping down beside him. Now that we're in eighth grade, we don't have to worry too much about the bus. Most of the mean older kids have dropped out, or they drive themselves to school now. It's unbelievable what a difference this makes in our lives. I asked Jimmy, "Did you study for the history test?"

"Nah," he grinned. "Do I ever?" This is true. Jimmy never seems to study for anything, and he still pulls pretty decent grades. Luke used to be the same way.

Then there's me, who spends hours on homework every night, trying to be the Perfect Student. I have no clue why. My parents always tell me to just do my best; they don't expect anybody to be perfect. They say I'm too hard on myself. Apparently they didn't need to punish me with time outs when I was little. All they had to do was look real mad, and I'd freak. Come to think of it, this still works.

Speaking of intimidation, Brandy Johnson got on the bus next. "Hi, Tom," she smiled. "Hi, Jimmy." She practically purrs when she talks. She slid into the seat in front of us.

Jimmy said, "Hey, Brandy," and nudged my elbow.

"Uh, hi," I mumbled, looking down at the dusty floor of the bus. Brandy turned back around, and her blond hair hung over the back of her seat, right in front of me. I felt like touching it. I wouldn't pull it or anything, but it just looked so…soft.

Brandy is one of the few kids from school who hasn't treated me any differently since Luke died. At first, everybody looked at me like I was handicapped. Their pity was sickening, and it made me nervous. After awhile, it got somewhat better, but luckily Jimmy and my other friends, along with the ever-flirtatious Brandy, have remained their normal weird selves. Most of the teachers have been cool, too, since they knew Luke and all. A couple of them have said I could talk to them if I was ever depressed or something. It's nice of them, but I can't see myself doing it. Besides, I could always talk to my parents.

Anyway, Brandy is nice and all, but she's really pushy. I can't say much to her because I'm afraid I'll babble like an idiot. She's got an awesome body and that gorgeous long blond hair. She could easily pass for eighteen. Rumor has it that she goes to the bars on the weekends with her mother, and they pick up men together.

The bus rolled into town, then to the Middle School, where I am finally in the oldest class. I had looked forward to it ever since Luke told me how great it was. And it is pretty awesome, being almost in high school. Of course, next year we'll be the babies again, but Luke said it's different in high school. He said everybody's more mature, and people are friends with kids who aren't even in their grade.

For the millionth time in the past six months, I wondered how I would get through life without Luke doing things first and telling me about them. I know it's selfish, but I was so used to him giving me all the details before I went in—to school, sports, camp, just about every experience I'd had. It scared me, knowing I was going into situations blind. Now I'll be the first to drive, go to college, have sex, get married (assuming I'll do all of those things; right now, none are looking too promising).

Luke always gave really useful advice, too—not like parents, who say things like, "Be sure to carry extra money with you in case of emergencies," or, "Wash your hands when you get off the school bus—who knows what kind of germs are in there?"

Not Luke. He'd say, "Don't sit on your backpack on the bus. It'll smash your lunch," or, "Stay away from Ron Gazdag. He spits at people who stare at his buck teeth." Now that's practical information.

Luke made it through almost a year of high school before he got killed in a car accident. He had stayed after school for track practice and was riding home with a kid from our neighborhood. Jake, a sophomore, had just gotten his driver's license. He pulled out in front of a semi. They were both killed instantly. Some of my dad's friends from the department said so, which I guess was supposed to make us feel better. It didn't.

Anyhow, in that time, Luke was Homecoming Prince, Freshman Class President, Lineman of the Year in football, and he got a 3.5 GPA. It's almost like he knew he didn't have much time in this life. He had tons of energy.

My first class is history, which was fine on this day, because I wanted to get my test over with. Mr. Duke passed out the tests, and I saw that there was a large essay section. I groaned. I hate essay questions. It's so much easier to do true and false or multiple choice (without too many choices, of course).

I glanced at Jimmy, and he gave me his "no problem" look. He smiled broadly. I picked up my pencil and thought, *let's get it over with.*

The test went OK, and the rest of the school day was uneventful. At lunch, I ate pizza in the cafeteria and talked about girls and football (well, mostly girls) with my friends. It's kind of dumb because guys always say they're "going out" with some girl, when none of us can drive yet. They might be a couple, but they don't actually go anywhere. They just hang out at school together. I haven't officially "gone out" with anybody yet, but I have some definite prospects. I have some girl friends, too. My parents say that the best couples start out as friends first.

After school I headed for football practice, my favorite part of the day. I'm no Brett Favre, but Coach Haskill says I have a super attitude and am a hard worker. I actually enjoy hitting the most. It's like I turn into somebody else, somebody who's mean and aggressive and tough. Growing up with Luke, I had to defend myself, and I really think it helped me.

In the hitting line, I bashed into Josh Moorlag, who, I personally think, has a big mouth. Plus, he thinks he's the hottest guy who ever walked the planet, if you know what I mean. He really thinks he's all that. He struts around school, and the girls act like he's one of the Backstreet Boys or something. It's very aggravating to us normal people.

I hit Josh, driving my shoulder into his, knocking him sideways. It felt good. He swore and shouted, "What are you doing, Schmidt? Save it for the game. I'm on your side, for God's sake."

"Sorry," I said, but I was grinning under my mouth guard. A guy like Josh needs to be taken down a peg or two. Jimmy gave me a thumbs-up from across the line.

Coach Haskill said, "Good hit, Schmidt."

To Josh he said, "Whatsa matter, Moorlag? Can't take a hit? I thought we raised our boys tougher in this town." Josh seethed silently.

After showers, my mom was waiting to pick me up in the car. We don't have a van anymore. I climbed into the front seat, and she said, "How was your day?" She had this fake frozen smile on her face, which looked as if you could chip it off with an ice pick.

"Great. How was yours?" I asked. Since I was pretty wound up from practice, I felt reasonably happy. It's hard to admit to myself when I feel good, because it seems traitorous to Luke.

Honestly, though, I'm sure he would want us to be happy. I've thought about it, and I definitely would want my family to go on and be happy without me. I wouldn't want them to suffer the way we have been in the past six months. Also, Luke was a very positive thinking person, up most of the time.

"It was...OK," she said slowly. I could tell she had something on her mind.

"What's wrong?" I asked, not knowing what to expect.

She cleared her throat, not a good sign. "Tom, I went to the doctor today after school," she said quietly, then looked down. She hadn't even started the car yet.

I felt myself starting to sweat worse than I had during football. Jesus, I thought, don't let her be sick. I'll do anything. I absolutely cannot lose one more person. "What's wrong, Mom?" I asked again, sounding kind of desperate.

"Nothing's wrong, really..." Her voice trailed off. Now she looked out the window. "It's just that...well, umm...I'm pregnant." She looked quickly at me for my reaction.

I just stared at her. I couldn't even think for a minute. I think I was in some kind of shock.

Mom said hastily, "This was not planned, Tom. It's a surprise, a shock, really, to Dad and me. I've been feeling kind of lousy, lately, but I figured it was stress, you know?" She searched my face for a response. I kept staring.

"Honey, you know we love you. And we love Luke. Nobody could ever take his place. You know that. But do you think you could learn to love a baby brother or sister? I realize it's a huge shock. You're fourteen now…"

I started to think then, and my first thought was how my mother got pregnant: uh-oh. I had to dismiss that thought from my mind fast before I hurled up my pizza. I mean, don't get me wrong. I know about sex and everything; I plan to have it someday myself. I just don't want to imagine my own parents doing it, you know?

A baby. Suddenly I smiled at her, a real smile. I was incredibly happy, and so relieved that my mother wasn't sick. My life was again clear. I was going to be the big bro, the boss, the advisor. Hell, I was probably going to be the babysitter. There would be four at the dinner table, one in a booster seat.

I yelled, "Yes!" I pounded my fist on the dashboard.

Jimmy heard me in the next car. His mom rolled down her window and said, "Everything all right over there?" Her eyes were concerned.

I rolled my window down, too. "Everything's fine, Mrs. Key," I replied. I grinned at Jimmy, saying, "I'll call you later." He nodded, looking bewildered.

Mom was staring at me, her eyes filled with tears (yes, again). "You're really excited?" she said, like she didn't quite dare to believe me.

She looked so hopeful. I hadn't seen that look in a long time. She continued, "I must say, you're taking the news better than your father. I called him at work, and he had to come home early to let it sink in. He couldn't concentrate." She giggled, kind of embarrassed.

"Mom, this is great news. No lie. I love babies." I paused, then said seriously, "Luke would be happy too. I'm sure of it. I have a feeling he's watching us now, and will watch the baby like a guardian angel. Kind of a bizarre angel, but…"

We laughed. "I'll tell it all about its other brother," I promised. I know I will. "Luke would be pumped to think of a little kid in the house. I'm just sorry he won't be here."

"Honey. He will be," she assured me. Her dark eyes were shining; she looked so young. I couldn't wait to get home and see Dad. I would high five him and say something profound like, "Cool!"

Isn't life weird? I turned on the car radio, and my mom and I sang "Livin' La Vida Loca" all the way home. We even picked up a pizza for supper, though my parents aren't usually into junk food. I didn't tell Mom that I'd had pizza for lunch. Actually, I could eat it three times a day for life and probably never get sick of it.

We talked all evening about the baby. My dad seemed to be getting somewhat used to the idea, especially when he saw how excited I was. He asked me if I'd help him with the baby, since I have considerably more energy that he does. I said, "Sure, except for diapers," which, for some reason, they thought was hilarious.

"All of this, including changing diapers, will be excellent training for the day you become a father," my mother told me.

"Who says I'm going to be a father?" I demanded, but they both just gave me with that "we know better than you do" look. Then they looked at each other in an extremely sappy way, if you know what I'm saying. My dad took my mom's hand and squeezed it. They sat there beaming at each other like they were the teenagers.

I rolled my eyes and excused myself to go call Jimmy, but actually, I didn't mind. I was glad we all had something to be happy about, to look forward to. Even though they can be kind of overly sentimental, my parents really are pretty great, for people of their age.

That night I dreamed about Luke. We were throwing passes in the front yard like we used to. Every time I went for one, Luke would yell, "Schmidt goes for the bomb!" When I caught the ball, he'd yell, "Touchdown! The crowd goes wild!" He'd cup his hands over his mouth and make these funny crowd noises.

The dream was so real. I woke up feeling renewed. My family would always be with me.

The Red Hat

Kay MacDonald

I celebrated my tenth birthday in October of 1948. My favorite gift was a red poplin hunting cap from my parents, and I am still amazed that they understood me so well.

I was not a girly girl. Chunky, freckled, sensible, braided-blonde hair, scabby knees, sun or wind burned cheekbones, I lived my life in the best imitation of my older brother, Cal, that I could muster. I wanted to be a boy.

This had nothing to do with wanting a penis. I think that I did not even know what one was, and if I had, I would have laughed at the idea. I just yearned to be a lean, flat, free male without all those encumbering bulges and rules made only for girls.

> **Kay MacDonald** lives with a trout fishing husband and three dogs in a fishing camp on a little river in northern Michigan. While working on two novels, she contributes feature articles to the *Traverse City Record Eagle's "Active Years"* magazine and won their *Summer Magazine* essay competition with her first entry.

"Oh, boy, thanks. This is a neat hat." I put it on for my family to see, and it settled down to the top of my ears, as if it were made for me. My mother smiled. My dad made a small amused mouth. My sister rolled her eyes. But Cal said, "You look great, Jeanie." I ate my chocolate birthday cake wearing the red hat and wasn't told to take it off, evidence that no one told boys what to do all of the time.

The next day, after school, I changed into Cal's old jeans and shirt, positioned the cap at a serious angle low on my forehead, called my dog, Skip, and went out to the field behind our house, where the cornstalks stood in teepee shaped shocks. Skip and I spent a lot of time in that field where in summer the corn grew in murmuring rows. We would hide in the tall acres of it. Now, in fall, it was an Indian village to me. Skip and I hollowed out one of the shocks and made a hideout every year.

Sometimes Sary, my next-door neighbor friend, came along, and that year she wore a cap too, her father's black and red-checked wool. But, as I knew she was never as serious about my adventure games as I was, I also knew that the cap was only a ticket into the game for her. For Sary was a real girl, and happy, too, in the midst of a gaggle of dolls. Usually it was just Skip and me and a sugar sandwich each.

My hat saw duty on rainy days when I spent hours loving the heft of the hammer, nailing things together in the garage. It saw duty, too, on hot days when I lay out under the grape arbor. It also served as a bowl to water Skip from Hogan's pump when Skip came along to watch me play softball with the boys on our road. My red hat kept the mosquitoes out of my hair in those sweaty games of hide-and-seek that we played on summer nights.

There was a bit of a mystery to those games. There were Sary and me, playing our little hearts out, thinking the point was to get in free, and there was Peggy of the Candy Mouth who had embarrassing bosoms. Peggy didn't seem to realize that one was supposed to get in to home as fast as possible without getting caught. She stayed out there in the dark for the longest times, and most of the boys were out there too.

"Jeanieee! Time to come in now!"

"Mom! Just a few minutes. Please."

"Now, Jean! It's 9:30."

So, with Skip on my heels, glad his body guard duties were over for the day, my red cap backwards on my sweaty head, I crossed the back yards to home. Peggy stayed out in the dark to play her version of the game. I knew just how my mother would sound over my protests.

"You are not Peggy, Jean. Girls have rules, and one of them is that you are in the house at a decent hour." Female rules, darned female rules.

The cap kept me good company for a long time--through winters when I skated and built snow forts and made break-neck sled runs down Larson's hill; and in the early springs when Skip and I could be back in the fields of corn stubble. I loved it when things began to green and turn moist where frogs lived and where violets grew in our secret place under the apple tree.

The hat saw me through the terrible loss of that good dog, Skip, and hid my eyes when I climbed the cherry tree to cry. It bore the teeth marks of the new puppy, Buff, who could never walk in Skip's pawprints. Buff met her death under a car before she finished growing. I still longed to be a boy, but I was beginning to see that there were rules of nature whether you were male or female.

The first day of junior high, I started for the bus in a hated navy blue skirt and fresh white blouse. My mother patted my cheek and said, "You look so nice, Jeanie. Your haircut makes you all grown up." I smiled bravely, but I hated my fuzzy home perm curls. When I got home from that big, tough new school, I wet my hair down, slicked it back furiously, slammed my red hat on my head, and stomped out into the fields, wishing Skip was with me.

My mother began to make small remarks about it being time to get rid of my cap, time to wear a kerchief or one of those cutesy stocking caps. But I loved the chewed bill and faded red crown and kept the cap on a hook in my own closet. I wore it every chance I had that autumn, my favorite time of year. I rode my bike and played ball harder than ever. I walked in the fields, but I was lonely, as Sary was spending more time with Peggy, and I missed a dog. I had trouble imagining that I was Robin Hood or Jessie James. I spent a lot of time just outside wearing my hat, defiantly ignoring the new and wondrous television set.

On the way to the bus one morning, as Peggy was rolling up her waistband to shorten her skirt, she asked, "You going to the Scout dance?" I looked at her in disbelief.

"Well, are you?" She practiced her pouty mouth for me.

"Are you kidding? I'd rather eat a snake's butt."

"Oh, come on. It'll be fun."

"I'm not going to any dumb dance. I can't dance and I don't wanta learn."

She eyed me speculatively. "We could get some of that frizz out of your hair with salad dressing. And you could leave your glasses off."

"Can't see without em."

"You don't hafta see," she giggled. "Just feel. Come on, Jeanie. My ma won't let me go without you. She says you're safe."

"Gee thanks. Safe. Frizzy hair. Glasses."

"You come down at 6:30, and I'll help you put on some lipstick. Hurry up. There's the bus." She took off with her silly girl's run, bouncing all over the place. I could beat her to the bus on one leg.

"Okay. But I'll hate it. You'll owe me."

I had scarlet fever when I was four and spent three weeks in the Pest House, an annex to the hospital that housed contagious patients. Once I fell off my bike while riding one handed in a spectacular crash of milk bottles and gravel and bare knees. Another time, I lied to my dad about the theft of my mother's valentine candy and suffered months of guilt and recrimination.

But none of these events amounted to anything, compared to the suffering I went through that whole week dreading that stupid Friday-night dance. Peggy talked about it non-stop. My mother and sister acted like they were going, too, as excited as they were. Finally, I got out of the house with my hat and my bike and rode hard to the woods where girls were not supposed to go. With tears running down my face, I climbed a tree and sat with my back against the trunk. I didn't know whether they were sad tears for Skip, or angry tears because no one would just let me be.

All day Friday I was sick to my stomach. Even Cal, coming to my rescue after supper, couldn't lift my dread. "Hey, it'll be okay. You're tough. You can do this standing on your head. You might even have fun. Then, Saturday, I'll take you to Sully's in the hot rod. Deal?"

"Deal . . . Cal. Thanks."

I wore my saddle shoes with white sox rolled down into a fat sausage around my ankles, and a blue plaid-pleated skirt with my sister's baby-blue pullover. It reeked of her perfume, and I felt silly and artificial. She did fix my hair in a sort of pageboy that was an improvement on the fuzz. When I got to Peggy's house, she looked me over. "Hey, you look neato." But it didn't lift my gloom. When she held my chin and coated my lips with her pink lipstick, I felt worse. She bubbled, and there was no question that she was a girl, with her big brown eyes peaking out from under her cheerful brown curls, and her pink-puffed lips giggling and chattering. I wanted to be at home in my jeans and my safe red cap. But this was all irreversible, and we were on our way in Peggy's dad's car.

Walking into the school with her was like being swarmed by a cloud of big brown gnats. The boys were lying in wait, and their hands were on her arms, begging her attention.

"Peggy."

"Hey, Peg."

"Dance with me first, Peg?"

"No, me, Peggy."

"Peggy, you're so pretty." She lavished her dimples on all of them and they trailed her in, the odor of their sweat mixed, tonight, with their dads' aftershave.

A lot of my friends were there, standing in little knots, busily talking, as if nothing were more important than seeing each other for about the tenth time that day. The music started from a scratchy Victrola, and everyone's breathing speeded up. Smiles grew rigid. Bracelets on wrists became fascinating. I wanted to go outside and play basketball with those boys I rough-housed with every day, but they weren't the same boys. They had combed hair. Their shirts were tucked in. Their shoes shone. They weren't approachable.

Then, the girls around me were murmuring with a bright awareness that raised their eyebrows and made their lips fuller. I felt like someone who didn't understand the rules of the game. Elizabeth and Suzanne were grinning at me as a boy's voice spoke into my ear, and a big hand closed over my elbow. I turned in confusion to look into the round, sweet face of Dickie Porter, the new boy on our bus. He was so tall that he bent toward me, and I looked up into his wide blue eyes. "Dance with me?" I couldn't hide.

I knew my face was red, and my smart mouth was failing me. "Uh . . . I . . . I don't. I can't . . . dance."

I heard a high laugh behind me and an, "Oh, Jeanie!"

He smiled. His lips were unboyishly soft over small neat white teeth. "I can show you. It's easy. Come on." Then he had his arm around my waist, his hand held mine, and there was no place for my other hand except on his shoulder. He ducked his head over mine and said, "That's right. See? Now just go where I go. How old are you?"

I whispered into his sweater front, "Twelve. Are you? Twelve, I mean."

"Nope. I'm thirteen. My name's Dickie Porter. You're Jeanie Sloan, right?" I could only nod.

"I see you riding your bike and playing ball. You're no sissy girl, are you? I like tough girls. I knew I'd like you when I saw you slide into home plate."

I was sinking, sinking into his soft tan sweater. He was so warm, and his arm on my waist felt real and good. I dared a quick look up, and his skin was like thick cream, his eyelashes longer than mine. He grinned and winked at me. My heart slammed into my chest like a kick, and he doubled the blow by whispering, "This is nice. You smell good. Let's not dance with anybody else."

And we didn't. I could feel his legs against mine in his corduroy pants, and I was sure he could feel the tremor in my skin that was born right in the pit of my stomach. I didn't even know my friends were watching in amazement. I just wanted to move slowly like this, back and forth, across the old creaking floor forever, thinking, "This is what it's like to be a girl." The room was brightly lit, but I felt like it was just the two of us dancing in the dark.

Peggy glided by in some boy's embrace and woke me with a punch. "Way to go, J!"

And my friend Dorothy mouthed, "He's cute" in an elaborate pantomime.

I couldn't even remember to pretend that I couldn't have cared less.

At home, in bed under my Wild West bedspread, I lay with my arms wrapped tight around myself, my skin fragile and newborn. In the dark, Dickie Porter's blue eyes made little lightning strikes, as I heard him again and again ask me to sit with him on the bus on Monday.

At breakfast, my dad handed out weekend chores, and my mother said, "Jeanie, don't fill your mouth so full. Try and eat like a lady." I grinned because I knew, now, that being a girl didn't have one single thing to do with table manners.

The rest is all just boring stuff. I sat with Dickie Porter on the bus Monday morning, and he was showing off like some boys did for Peggy: talking too loud, shoving some kids out of the way. We sat together for maybe two weeks, and held hands a little, and someplace along the line, he found Sylvy Hansen, who was definitely not tough at all. But, by that time, Doug Wiseman had told me he thought I was sort of cute, and I ate that bait right up. He even kissed me one afternoon behind the bus.

I found my red cap the next spring, when I was under orders to clean my closet or have it burned out. I felt sort of disloyal, and then I felt sad when it made me think of Skip. So I hung it up high on a hook, and it was there when I left for college.

Sometimes, now, I wish I knew where it was. I think that if I put it on and went outside, Skip would show up, and things would be safe and good --the way they were before I knew I was a girl.

Eternal Love

Linda Lou Costa

I remember when I was a little girl, it was such a special treat to go to Grandma's house. This particular weekend I want to share with you is a story I will never forget.

It rained from the time I got there, and I was tired of playing inside. I was ten at the time and wasn't very interested in putting together the puzzle Grandma wanted us to put together. I was always talking and laughing. Grandma said I was good for her; she loved to hear me laugh. Like most ten-years-old, I loved to ask a lot of questions, and this day was to be no different.

> **Linda Lou Costa** was born and reared in Detroit, Michigan, and moved to Indiana in 1989 where she works as a secretary in her church. This is her first attempt at writing for publication. Linda enjoys traveling and is an avid reader.

"Grandma?" I asked, "How come I don't have a Grandpa?"

Grandma didn't answer; she just sat there staring at the puzzle piece in her hand. I thought I might have asked a wrong question, so I quickly said, "I'm sorry I asked. I won't ask again."

Grandma looked at me and must have seen the remorse in my eyes because she gave me one of her warm smiles, and said, "No, Beth, it's okay that you asked. I can't believe I have never mentioned him to you."

"Will you now, Grandma?" I asked eagerly.

"On a day like this, it seems fittin' to talk about your Grandpa. Let's get some milk and cookies, and go into the living room. There's something in there that I want to show you."

After going into the living room, Grandma went to the hutch in the corner and opened the bottom drawer. She pulled out a small box and came to sit next to me on the couch. Grandma opened the box, pulled out a picture and said, "Here is a picture of your Grandpa."

I took the picture with all the care that I had because I knew this was important to my Grandma. I looked at the picture, then looked at Grandma, and told her, "Grandma, you sure are funny. This is a picture of my daddy."

"No, Beth," she calmly stated, "this is a picture of your Grandpa, but your daddy looks a lot like him, too."

"Oh! Why is he wearing that funny looking hat? Where did you meet him? What was he like?" I started asking.

"Hold on, little one! One question at a time. How about if I start at the beginning? I think I will answer all of your questions."

"Okay, Grandma."

We sat quietly on the couch before Grandma started her story. "I'm going to take you back to a time, long ago. The year was 1940, when your Grandma was eighteen years old. I know you didn't think Grandma was ever young, but I was once."

I looked over at Grandma and covered the smile on my mouth as she continued. "We were having a box social at church. That is where a young girl makes a picnic lunch for two, and a young man bids on the box that contains the lunch. Then the girl and boy eat the picnic lunch together. More than likely the young man knows whose box he is bidding on. I didn't want to go to this particular box social because my beau and I just broke up, and I didn't want to see him bidding on someone else's box; but my mom insisted that I go. She said, 'It will do him good to see what kind of a lunch he is missing out on.' My mom fixed the box and added a ribbon to the box that matched the ribbon in my hair.

"We were off to the church. When we got there, I didn't want to go inside, but then I saw my friends, and they talked me into it. The time came for the bidding, and my box was the first one to be auctioned. I was so scared no one would bid on it, but they did.

"It started out at 50 cents, and someone in the back said, 'One dollar.'

"Then the first boy said, 'A dollar fifty.'

"The boy in the back said, 'Two dollars.'

"This continued between those two, until the boy in the back of the church bought my box for five dollars. My box received the highest bid that night.

"When the boy came forward to claim his box, I saw him for the first time. Oh, Beth, he was the most handsome man I had ever met! He was in his Navy uniform. That was his Naval hat he was wearing in this picture. When I met him, he reached for the box, and introduced himself as 'Ensign Andrew Davis of the United States Navy, at your service, ma'm.' He escorted me outside to the front lawn of the church, and we talked the entire time. I told him I never heard of anyone bidding so much money for a box lunch before, and he said he only did it because he wanted to meet me so much. Andrew noticed that the ribbon in my hair matched the one on the box and said he would have paid ten dollars if he had to, just to meet me.

"Because it was early fall, it got chilly in the evenings. I had forgotten my coat, so Andrew offered me his coat. He was the gentleman every girl dreams of meeting. He walked me home that night, and the next afternoon he was at my house, asking my dad if he could court me. Because my dad liked what he saw in Andrew, and was impressed that Andrew asked for his permission, he gladly gave it. We saw each other every day for the next three weeks.

"Finally it came the day we both dreaded. Andrew received his orders. Although he was only going to a neighboring state, we still wouldn't see each other every day like we had been. We promised to write each other once a day and mail the letters at the end of the week. We kept our promise to each other, and our letters to each other were what kept us going throughout our separation.

"One day, upon receiving Andrew's letters, I started crying. My mother came in to see what was wrong, and I told her that Andrew was coming for a short visit. I couldn't wait! After months of waiting to see him again, it was finally happening. The days slowly went by until Andrew's return. Was I ever surprised when Andrew showed up a day early! We talked for hours before he said that he needed to go. Andrew had already prearranged to talk to my dad, so it looked so natural for Andrew and my dad to walk outside together.

"Beth? Did you want some more milk and cookies?" Grandma asked.

"Grandma, I can't think about eating right now. Please tell me more of the story," I asked.

"Okay, sweetie, Now let's see where did I leave off? Oh, yes, my dad and Andrew outside talking. I wondered what he was saying to my dad. He looked so serious and nervous through the window as I peeked from behind the curtain. Andrew later told me about the conversation. He started by telling my dad how much he loved me, and he was wondering, since he would only be in town for one week, if we could get married. He went on to tell Dad that he had an apartment all picked out for us near the base. Andrew said he was so nervous trying to persuade my father, that he never head my dad say, 'Yes!' Finally, after my dad couldn't take any more of Andrew's talking, my dad grabbed him by the shoulders and told him, 'You better go ask Elizabeth before I change my mind.'"

Grandma stopped talking at this point. She just looked down at the picture of Grandpa and ran her finger over his face. I waited patiently for what seemed to be hours before I blurted out, "Well, you told him no, didn't you? One week to plan a wedding isn't a long time, Grandma."

Grandma looked over at me, with a smile, and replied, "You're right, Beth. One week to plan a wedding isn't a long time, but I did get married two days later without a big, fancy wedding. We moved into the apartment that Andrew had rented near the base, and I loved being married. Four months after were married, I found out I was going to have a baby – your daddy. Life couldn't have been better for us. But our happiness was short-lived when Andrew received his new orders. He was to be stationed on the battleship *Arizona*, at Pearl Harbor, Hawaii. Your Grandpa was scheduled to leave the day after Thanksgiving, and I was not allowed to go with him. After talking it over, we both agreed it would be best for me to move back to my parent's house.

"We shared a tearful goodbye at the train station with other families standing nearby, saying goodbye to their loved ones, too. Andrew rode the train to California and then caught a plane to take him to Hawaii; he would arrive there on December fifth. Again, we both promised to write every day while we were away from each other.

"Then it came – December 7, 1941. My mother and I were doing some sewing in the living room. We were listening to the radio when an announcer interrupted the program for a special news bulletin." With a catch in her throat, Grandma continued. "He said that Pearl Harbor has just been attached by Japan. Just then my dad came running in the house. After seeing the look on our faces, he knew we already heard the news. He came to me and said that it didn't mean Andrew was hurt; we would just have to wait to find out. I couldn't say anything. I put down my sewing; and when I started to stand up, I fainted. It was a good thing that Dad was there because he carried me to my room and then went for the doctor.

"My parents feared I would lose the baby because of the news I heard on the radio. The doctor told them that I was to stay in bed, and he would be by the next morning to check on me. My mother stayed with me the whole night. We heard early the next morning that the *Arizona* had been sunk, and many of our sailors had died in the attack. The doctor came in the morning as he promised and told me that as long as I took care of myself, the baby and I would be fine. He gave me something to make me sleep; he told me sleep was the best thing for me right then.

"Day after day went by, and I could assume only the worst. It was a week later when we received the news we were dreading. Andrew was among the 1,177 men who went down with the *Arizona*. I never thought I would recover from such a loss as that – my only true love was gone! I was hurting so much. I cried all the time. Well, four months later your dad was born, and I named him

Andrew Davis, after his dad. With the help of my parents, I raised him the best that I could."

"Grandma, why didn't you ever marry again?" I asked.

"Because, Beth, it wouldn't be fair to a future husband. You see, I loved my husband, your Grandpa, so much that I knew I could never love another man. You know, Beth, I don't think I ever did get over his death, so deep is my love for your Grandpa. Andrew was my one true mate for life, and I will remain his for all time. I could never love and share my life with another man."

"Oh, Grandma, that is such a romantic, but sad, story. I wish I could have known him."

"I wish you could have too, sweetheart, because then he would still be with us today," Grandma said smiling. "There's one more thing I want to show you, Beth, but you have to promise never to tell anyone about this. Promise?"

"I promise, Grandma," I answered.

Grandma got off the couch and walked over to the hutch again. She opened the bottom drawer and pulled out another box. This box was bigger than the other one. I thought it was more pictures. She placed the box on her lap and then opened it. To my surprise, there were no pictures, but letters – hundreds of letters. Then Grandma explained, "I was so used to writing to your Grandpa that after he died, I never stopped. I write him every day like we promised, and then I put the letter in an envelope at the end of the week. These are all my letters to him over the years. I tell him everything that is happening, and by doing that I feel like he is here with us. I have told him all about you, too, Beth, just like I have told you about him."

"Grandma, that is so neat. Thank you for telling me about my Grandpa. I promise your secret is safe with me," I told her with tears in my eyes.

Grandma neatly put all her things back into her boxes and put them away in the hutch. We then went out to the kitchen and had some more cookies. That day at Grandma's was the best because that was the day I got to know my Grandpa.

Loathe Thy Neighbor

Fred Thornburg

Six o'clock came, and six o'clock went. This wasn't the first Sunday that had ended in tension for Pete. The day had started out as a relaxed "Norman Rockwell" Sunday, but by the afternoon, it had turned into an "Archie Bunker" Sunday. Jackie and the kids had taken off around three, with Pete running alongside the car screaming at them to stay put. Three hours, he'd told them. Be back in three hours, or don't come back at all. Yet here he was, standing at the end of the driveway, alternately staring up the road and down at his watch. His face was heating up again as the anger reawakened. He swore out load as he stormed back toward the house.

> **Fred Thornburg** has been writing for years for his own satisfaction. He has gained some confidence from small articles published locally, but received a real boost by being accepted in the first volume of *Voices of Michigan.* Being published has encouraged Fred to continue looking for ordinary stories he can twist slightly.

"Pete, I've got a minute, if you wanna talk. I couldn't help but notice you out here losing your composure."

Pete narrowly refrained from rushing his elderly neighbor, Lou, as he shuffled across their front lawns. A three-mile dead-end road, two houses on it, and they have to be side by side, Pete thought. Worse than that, Lou and Sue would not stay inside, and could not keep their nose out of Pete's affairs. Since their retirement, it seemed like they were always outside, either mowing or trimming, or coming and going in the car.

One thing Pete knew, they rarely missed one of his arguments with Jackie. When Lou and Sue--or as Pete referred to them, the *Oooh* twins--were out, they were hugging and laughing as if to rub their relationship in Pete's face. They reminded him of news clips of President and Mrs. Bush at their beach house. Pete barely refrained from using the "f" word on Lou as he told him he was okay.

"Well, if you change your mind, swing by. Our door is always open. Sue and I have been married fifty-two years now. We've had a few fights, not as vocal as yours, but they're mostly forgotten. We've settled into a predictable routine, you might say. I guess like an infant needs routine and gets cranky if disrupted from it, so it goes with us old folks. I gotta get going. It's pizza and "60 Minutes" tonight. If you want some advice, catch us in the yard or drop in any weeknight at seven for tea and the "Wheel." I, uh, I may be presumptuous here, but it seems like every time you storm out of your house like this, you compromise your integrity. Once you recoup, how about stopping by? Take care, buddy."

Buddy, Pete thought. Don't give me that buddy shit. A buddy wouldn't talk to Jackie while I'm at work, telling her how good she could have it, and how incompetent her husband appears. A buddy would mind his own business. Pete wasn't so sure the *Oooh* twins weren't the cause of so much tension between him and Jackie. She saw them as the explicit example of how a marriage could and should be: routine, doors always open. He'd like to take them down a notch or two. He now had double aggravation. As he watched the *Oooh* twins pull out of their drive in the *Oooh* mobile, his mood turned from aggravation to anticipation.

The dead-end road was once again silent, as a slight grin surfaced on Pete's face. He started towards the *Oooh* Home of Ideal Relationships in a lighter mood. Had he not been doubly angered, he never would have had such thoughts. If Lou would've minded his own business, Pete would not be standing in their opened garage. Lou hadn't lied; the door was open. Pete stood in the breezeway with three options: turn and go home undiscovered, toss a match, then turn away, or just have a peek around.

He found he was still too mad for the first scenario, not yet mad enough for the second, and if he did just cruise around, what would that hurt? His anger was subsiding; his curiosity was up. He was a ten-year-old kid again, exploring his parents' closet, or the janitor's office at school. He was sure he would find evidence of some hidden secret life. Maybe find something illegal, immoral. Something that he could store in the back of his mind for future reference. Something that would bring them down a notch. He hadn't found anything then, and he didn't now. No treasure in this castle. Reluctantly he turned to go. It was true. They were the perfect couple. Everything was in place; this house was ruled by routine. Then the plan came clear to Pete. Routine would be their downfall.

Their routine was the exact opposite of his stress. They had no stressful career. They weren't raising two kids in these difficult times. They weren't too worried about money. No wonder they don't fight; they don't have stress. Yet. Pete looked around and decided to give them a little. It had to be subtle, though. Too much disturbance would look fake, and they'd know someone had been in their house. He'd cause some disorder under the surface. Yeah, pit them against each other.

He turned and walked into the kitchen. This would be easy. He went through the list of things he knew he was guilty of at his house, things that irritated Jackie. He turned on the almost-empty coffee maker. He washed all the milk down the sink, then replaced the empty carton on the top shelf. He took a piece of last night's broiled fish and dropped it behind the gas range. He found the bread drawer and stuck the little twisty in his pocket, allowing the bread some air. He took off two steps at a time up the stairs toward the bedroom. For the first time in a long time, he was having fun. He set the time on the clock radio on Lou's nightstand back fifteen minutes, then turned it on, so he could change the station to heavy metal. He left it off with the volume cranked up and the alarm set for three in the morning. He moved the bookmark in Sue's book up a few pages. He went into the bathroom off their bedroom and had some more fun. Pete turned the hot water faucet handle off as hard as he could, and then turned it past it's normal stopping point. When he spun it back around, and then turned it off, it let loose with a slow, steady drip. Perfect. He took an oversized wad of toilet paper and formed it into a tight ball and flushed it down the stool. The water rose up only slightly inside the bowl. It would trickle in until it looked normal, and the next flush would send it overflowing. Pete ran back down the stairs thinking that living well wasn't the best revenge; revenge was the best revenge.

The possibilities seemed endless, but Pete figured he could be running short on time. Too many more setups could expose him. He had done a lot in a little time, but he was confident that this ten-minute's worth of pranks would take days to be totally revealed. In a better mood than he had been in for some time, he bounded out of the *Oooh* castle, leaving the door open behind him.

Jackie and the children returned to the smell of a fresh-baked cake around eight that night. Pete apologized and seemed like a new man to Jackie. A changed man. A man with a mission. And that he was. Over the next few days, Pete sneaked next door every chance he got. He left shoes on the front porch in the rain. He took dirty clothes out of their hamper and threw them down on the closet floor. He plugged the upstairs stool again. He erased messages on the answering machine. Always a little, never too much. He tried to keep it discreet enough so it would stay in the back of their minds--stored with the things that irritate you a little, yet not so much that they become an issue on their own. But given enough, they avalanche. Things were going Pete's way.

On Friday, Jackie called Pete at work, wondering if he would mind going next door at lunch time to help Lou move the gas range. It seemed there was a bad stench coming from behind it. Jackie didn't pick up on the laugh that was mixed in with the "Yes." He told her he'd be there at noon.

A slight smirk twisted on Pete's lips as he knocked on the screen door. It stank, all right: smelled like rotted fish mixed with the perspiration of obnoxious do-gooders who were sweating the small stuff. "Lou, Sue, how are you two?" Pete half sang and half yelled into the kitchen hallway after letting himself in. He was getting used to it.

"Pete, thanks for stopping by. I can't move the stove by myself, and we think that's where that fowl smell is coming from," Lou said, as he set a pair of pliers on top of the stove.

That's not fowl, Pete thought; it's fish. He had noticed it getting worse, and was surprised they had waited this long to address it. "No problem, buddy. Other than that awful stench, how is it going? You look and sound kinda down. Anything I can help you with? You and Sue having problems? Need to talk, buddy?"

He grabbed the pliers off the top of the stove to keep them from falling, and started to swing the stove back and forth, slowly walking it out. He was listening to Lou go down the list of things that had happened lately. He was making mental check marks as he went. There was a handful that they had not gotten to yet. Pete slid down between the range and the wall as Sue entered the room. Pete said hello, and asked her for a bag for what appeared to be an old piece of fish.

"I tell you, Pete, this piece of rotted fish pretty much sums up this last week. It was a stinker, to be sure." This was music to Pete's ears. "But you know, like this fish, no matter how bad the problem stinks, we deal with it. The problems we had last week were small, yet they added up. I guess old age is catching up with us. But Sue and I look back and laugh. This past week has brought us closer. We've worked side by side and deepened our bond. Maybe that's the key. You know, maybe you and Jackie should try working through your difficulties as a team. Look at what life throws you not as dilemmas, but as opportunities. Work through them together and become stronger."

Pete couldn't believe what he was hearing. Fifteen minutes ago he had been elated; now he was devastated. He hadn't driven a wedge between them, he'd coated them with glue. Not only that, they had the audacity to throw it back at him. He was threading the brass connector back on the line so he could shove the stove back in. He had to control his temper, as over tightening it could, could what? Cause a slight tear in the fragile copper line running between the shut-off valve and the range inlet? Then what would happen to Mr. and Mrs. *Oooh Got All The Answers?* He tightened it, then over tightened it, until it started to give and cut all the way through. He could not hear or smell a leak, but his fingers could feel a slight breeze as the gas escaped. The fish pungency would hang heavy for some time. He slid the range back, paying little attention to what Sue and Lou were jabbering about. That is, until Sue came out with a large candle and a silver Zippo lighter.

"No!" Pete shouted.

This startled Sue. "What's the matter, Pete? You're looking at me like I'm carrying a bomb. I just thought a candle might absorb that stench. That's all. Why'd you shout at me so?"

"No, don't light that candle. No, I mean, what with the week Lou has described to me, I hate to see you press your luck. Don't you have some spray or something?" All the while Pete was backing toward the door.

"I know," rang in Lou, "we were going to have ring bologna and kraut tonight anyway. I'll go downstairs and bring up the crock and let it breath here in the kitchen. You ever had any of our home-made sauerkraut before, Pete?"

Pete was almost in the garage and anxious to leave. "No, I never have. I'd like to try some, one of these days. Hey, sorry, but I've got to run. Don't want to be late to work, you know. Not all of us are retired. See you two later, maybe. Bye."

Pete hurried to his car and took off back to work. He felt a slight twinge of resentment, but it was overshadowed by a feeling of relief. A small fire would make them appear unable to stay on their own. They would be forced to reside elsewhere: new neighbors. A big fire, and, well, there would be only one house on this dead end road: no neighbors.

Pete spent the afternoon torn. He could do the right thing, call Lou casually and tell him to throw some soapy water on the connection and check for a gas leak. There would indeed be one. He would then tell Lou to turn it off, and he could fix it tonight. He would look like a hero. On the other hand, there was a very good chance that he could wind up with different neighbors. Or no neighbors. It would look like nothing but an accident. Pete was leaning towards the latter scenario. The *Oooh* couple had been a thorn in his side for years now. They were one of many sources of stress, one of the major sources. In fact, until this whole venture began, he had not had a break from stress. Now, for the first time in a long time, he looked forward to going home at night. His work seemed to be going smoother. In fact, he and Jackie had been getting along better than ever. Yes, for the first time in a long time, he had a hobby, albeit not necessarily a healthy one. Nonetheless, it was a hobby, and as hobbies go, what fun is it to build a model rocket if you never follow through and launch it? He'd gone this far. He decided to ride it out.

He pulled into his drive at six forty-five that night. The street still held two houses. Maybe they had discovered the leak and turned off the gas. More probable though, was that they had not started the stove yet. "Wheel Of Fortune" would be on at seven o'clock. The burner would be lit for tea right before "Wheel" started. Pete kicked off his shoes and pulled up a chair to get a good view of Lou's kitchen. He wondered where the rest of the family was, then thought how perfect it was that he could watch clearly without having to sneak around. He turned his TV on, with the volume down, just loud enough to hear the beginning of "Wheel's" familiar theme music. Keeping the *Oooh* bomb in sight, he went to the kitchen to get himself a cold celebratory beer.

He reached in and got the beer without ever taking his eyes off their house. The fireball exploded in the very instant the refrigerator door was closing. It shook Pete's kitchen so much that it dislodged a ladybug magnet, and its handwritten note, off the fridge door. The note floated to the linoleum floor and landed words up. The ink was barely dry on Jackie's articulate writing:

~~~

Pete, having tea and kraut with Sue and Lou. Swing over and join us. Jackie   xxooxx

The Whine Bottle

Timothy Lambert 'From an idea by Kristin Story'

It was with a great sense of expectation that I knocked on Professor Charles Dupre's front door one fateful day in June. The week before, he had sent me an e-mail, claiming a great discovery and offering my network an exclusive broadcast, after which, he said, "All hell would break loose." My own career had been a little slow of late. "In Depth" was still one of the top shows on the air, but I was one of six producers, and had not had a story broadcast for almost two months. I could use a blockbuster. In fact, I needed one.

> **Timothy Lambert** has spent most of his life as a professional musician. He has lived and worked in San Francisco, New York City, Vienna, Austria, and various other places. Tim currently performs at Grand Hotel on Mackinac Island, Michigan. He has written for radio and magazine.

Dupres lived in an old Victorian on top of Potrero Hill. The view from his front porch was a favorite of films and cop shows--you'd recognize it--and a favorite of mine, as well. The Bay Bridge, although three miles away, seemed to grow out of the crest of Rhode Island Street, one of those "only in San Francisco" tableaus the city is famous for. As I watched a few perfect clouds drift lazily over Oakland on their way to Sacramento, the door was flung open.

"David. Good to see you. Come in, please."

Shabby, disheveled, threadbare, ratty, (take your pick) any of these serve to describe Dupres' appearance. The familiar image of a distracted scientist in an oversized lab coat, complete with stains and torn pockets, ushered me into a large front room in which the messiness perfectly reflected the man's personality. There was stuff everywhere, in stacks and piles and mounds and clusters and heaps--too much for me to comprehend individually. I felt a general impression of the dusty back room of a museum somewhere, filled with acquisitions not yet displayed, catalogued or dealt with in any way. It was all I could do not to burst out of the door in a claustrophobic frenzy.

"Have a seat," he told me, but I didn't need to look to know that any chair in that room would be buried. Dupres understood, lifting a pile of books and dropping them on the floor. He placed a chair before me, and I sat. Not given to small talk, he began at once.

"David, what would you say if I told you that I've discovered the essence of emotions?"

"You mean why we feel excited or happy or bored?"

"Not why. How. I've discovered how to fool the brain into releasing the chemicals responsible for our emotions." He said much more, going on at length with a highly technical explanation that I could neither understand nor reproduce here.

I nodded my head, said, "Uh-huh," a few times, but it didn't matter to me. I'm not a science guy. The network had people for that. Suffice it to say that it sounded good, and I was interested. If his discovery worked as Dupres said it would, all hell would indeed break loose. It would be a huge feather in my cap to introduce it on "In Depth," and I told him so.

"I knew you'd be excited, David. Would you like to try one now?"

"Well, I'm not sure…" I said, but of course I wanted to. At least I think I did. I had to know if it worked or not, true, but…

"Oh, come now, of course you do," said the professor, rubbing his hands and smiling. "I suggest you pick an emotion you rarely feel, as a true test. How about rage?"

Rage was one I knew well and often felt. I live in a high-pressure world where little things have profound consequences. I often scream at people who make silly mistakes--mistakes that, in the costly arena of television production, can very quickly become very expensive. Rage would not do, and I said so.

"Well, then," said Dupres, "how about depression? I've known you a long time, David, and I've never seen you depressed."

That's because I hide it, I thought. I am often depressed. My personal life is a long line of mistake leading to blunder leading to disaster: a sad tale of misguided trust and bad decisions. Women intimidate and overpower me. I lose myself in them, and they sense this, an unfortunate situation with unhappy consequences. I was, in fact, depressed right then, due to…well, never mind, enough to say that depression wouldn't work either.

I don't complain, though. I'm not a whiner. Maybe I could try that?

"Charles, can you make me into a sniveling whiner, complaining about everything?"

"Certainly. Let me see, self-pity will do nicely. Number Fourteen, an excellent choice. Wait here, I'll get it."

He went downstairs to his laboratory, to return a moment later with a small bottle he placed in front of me. It's size and shape were that of a Tabasco sauce container, with a small amount of blue liquid inside. Dupres shook the bottle, removed the cork, filled a teaspoon with the elixir, and handed it to me.

"Drink up."

What am I to say about the next several minutes? The ability to control my emotions, never easy for me, would be a Godsend, completely foreign to my troubled nature. I tried to imagine never being depressed again, becoming happy, even sad, at will. It would be wonderful, I thought, not to be plagued by feelings I could not control, to be able to make thoughtful, rational decisions instead of stumbling into the emotional quagmires I normally blundered into. All this, and more, seemed heavenly to me. I pulled the magic potion, for it was nothing less, toward me.

Why, then did I hesitate?

Why didn't I just drink the stuff to see what would happen? I wasn't afraid. Or, to be more accurate, I was afraid. I must have been afraid of losing my lack of control. If I could conjure up an emotion from a bottle, what value would it have? Laughing or crying on demand would soon lose its thrill.

I suppose.

More importantly, I was afraid of being overpowered by my feelings, as I often am. This is something I've dealt with a lot, and it has, in fact, been a major factor in several of the breakups that sum up my relationships. I was going through one at the time. Knowing this, knowing how I felt about things, the anger and hurt and frustration and betrayal inside me, I worried that I would spend the next hour or so spewing out a wave of chemically induced self-pity. I sat unmoving, the drug inches from my mouth.

Dupres looked at me impatiently. "Well, go ahead. It won't bite."

"Ah, but if it works as you say, it will bite. Who else has taken this stuff? Is it safe?"

"Of course it's safe, " he insisted. "I've taken it, my assistant Ambrose has taken it, his friend Philip, and the list goes on, including over thirty people. No negative reactions, no side effects. Your emotions, whichever you choose, will be expanded for about eight hours, according to results so far. You will be Subject Number Thirty-two."

Dupres pulled a mini-cassette recorder out of his jacket. Saying, "Subject Thirty-two, vial fourteen, 2:35 P.M. June 8" into the device, he settled back in his chair. He had a "let's get on with it already" look on his face.

"Does it taste bad?" I asked him.

Irritated, he said, "It has no flavor and no odor. Shall I start the recorder now?"

"Well…"

"Oh, for God's sake, David, drink up. You'll be perfectly fine. On three. One-two…"

The potion had no aroma, as Dupres had said, but even so I held my nose, stuck the spoon in my mouth, and drank up.

Nothing happened. Not a thing. Why had I done this? I felt the same as always. Sitting in a chair in front of Dupres, I thought myself a fool. Come to think of it, the chair was not all that comfortable. I crossed my right leg over my left, hoping that would help, but it didn't. I worried my leg would wrinkle my trousers, so I straightened it out, which was no better, really. The back of the chair was digging into my own back, forcing me into sitting up straighter than I wished, so I slumped, but that was even worse. I said as much to Dupres.

"Yes, yes, I see. Go on," he replied, annoying the hell out of me. Who did he think he was, a shrink? I hadn't come here to be tut-tutted. Why hadn't I stayed at home today, or gone sailing, or done any of the thousands of things I could have done instead of sitting in this uncomfortable chair in this messy room opposite a crackpot inventor? That was when I noticed the light, a really annoying single bulb surrounded by a white Chinese paper lantern almost directly above my head. It was very bright and shone directly on my face.

"Could you lower the light please?" I politely asked. "It's hurting my eyes."

"I'm sorry, David, it's the only light in the room. It's not on a dimmer, and I must observe your reactions," he said unhelpfully. To his recorder he said, "Subject Thirty-two is beginning to complain about minor annoyances."

Well, what did he expect? Minor annoyance, indeed. Of course I will mention something that bothers me. I was, after all, his guest, wasn't I? Why wouldn't he want to make me more comfortable? What kind of hospitality was this, where you stuck a friend on a rickety old chair with a light glaring on his face? It was like a Gestapo interrogation. I'd been treated better when interviewing convicts in their cells, and I said so. I am a fairly important person, and I deserved some consideration.

Dupres nodded again, speaking quietly into his infernal tape recorder.

It was then that I noticed the music.

It had been playing since I'd come in, I realized--some kind of monotonic new-age gibberish, played by a barefoot pianist, one phrase repeated over and over and over and--you get the idea. Someone must have turned it up louder, as it began to assault my eardrums, horribly. I mean, it was really loud.

"Dupres, how can you work with that racket going on?"

"Racket? You mean the meditative music? I can barely hear it, but I'll turn it off, if you'd like."

"Yes, I would," I said gratefully. "It makes it difficult for me to think. Piano music affects me strongly."

"Oh?" Dupres walked over to a small stereo on a shelf and shut the music off, mumbling something into his recorder as he went. "How so?" he asked me.

"Well, if you must know…" I began, slowly realizing what was happening. "Angela played the piano, you know. She would spend hours at the keyboard, playing beautifully. I put a Steinway in my house just for her, and now she's gone."

"I see, go on. Who's Angela?"

Angela. How could he not know Angela? She had been the focus of my life the past sixteen months. My world revolved around her. My only desire was to please her, my only wish to keep her happy. Beautiful, sweet Angela. I did everything I could for her, gave her all my time, spent a small fortune on her, and for what? She had run off, just weeks before, with a musician I'd introduced her to. Younger, handsomer than me, probably richer, he had swept her off her feet, as if I'd never existed. I could not believe her coldness to me toward the end. I always tried to make excuses for her, to understand, to let it go, to try and find the compelling reason behind her meanness to me, to try to figure out what I'd done, or not done, to bring about her behavior. One day, she had simply gone away, leaving me high and, except for my constant tears, dry. I missed her. I loved her. I didn't want to live without her.

"You know, Professor," I said, taking my cell phone out of my pocket to call the network, "I think you're onto something here."

Grown-up Grouchies Go Away

Jodi Burkett

It was Saturday. Mom was in her usual work day hurry. That meant picking up stuff that didn't seem to bother anybody and cleaning stuff that looked fine, anyway. The grown-up grouchies were wrinkling her forehead.

"Mom, what's so important about getting the dishes done? Won't the sink be full again later? Just do them one time, later."

Mom shrugged and put the drooly casserole pan down.

But one minute later, Mom was in a hurry again. The grown-up grouchies were pinching her eyebrows. That must hurt.

I shook my finger at her, like she does at me when I bite my fingernails. "Mom, what's so important about straightening the house? Won't it be messy again later? Just do it one time. Later."

Mom shrugged and put down Dad's crunchy-dirty socks, my A+ spelling test, high heels, the remote controls, and a sandwich crust.

But one minute later, Mom was in her hurry again. The grown-up grouchies were making her eyes thin and her nose holes big, like a horse. She was working so hard; she even breathed like one.

> **Jodi Burkett** feels that we as adults are easily controlled by this high-speed world. We become automated, then enslaved. This shuts out the most important things in our lives, our children. It is their innocence that sets us free and keeps us young. Jodi writes to help children understand adults, and perhaps to help adults understand themselves.

With a loud breath, I shook my head at her. "Mom, what's so important about sweeping the floor? Won't it be messy after lunch and dinner? Just clean it one time. Later." Mom shrugged.

The dog hair and chips in the dustpan fell back on the floor. She put the broom back in the closet. But Mom was in her hurry, one minute later.

The grown-up grouchies were weighing down the corners of her mouth now. She reminded me of Grampa's old wooden puppets. My hands on my hips, I stepped right in front of Mom. "Mom, what's so important about all this stuff you find to do? You are not at work today, so stop working! Grown-ups need some playing, too. Just do it later!"

It was quiet for a whole long time. "But Connor, I have one more important thing I have to do right now," said Mom like a rock, if it could talk. Now I could feel those heavy grouchies land on my mouth. Hadn't she been listening to me? Mom stood up and turned to walk away. I closed my eyes. They felt as heavy as my mouth.

Suddenly, I felt a cool breeze on my face. I opened my eyes to see Mom spinning around, dropping the cleaner from her hand, and scooping me up in her arms. She tickled me and laughed, "Right now I have to play with my favorite toy, YOU!"

The rest of that Saturday felt like a no-homework night and summertime! There was magic in the mud bombs that covered us, and pixy-dust in the grass we threw. There was a super-hero power ruling the lands we rescued, and a monster appetite at dinner. Bedtime stories were more real, and snuggles warmer. Mom even told me stories from her head about when I was a baby. That's when I think I fell asleep.

But when I got up in the morning, I saw that the dishes were done, the house was straight, the floor was swept, and the counters wiped. There sat Mom in her robe with her coffee, reading a book. There were no wrinkles on her forehead, or thin, grouchy eyes, no horse breath nose or puppet mouth. Instead, she smiled at me with magic on her face from playing with her favorite toy.

Captain Gordon's Ghost

Randy Bernard

It was on a Saturday near Dead Drop Falls, that my friend, Amy, and I, came face to face with Captain Gordon's Ghost. We had been bored by city life and looked forward to this weekend getaway with Amy's parents. We longed for the wilderness and adventure. We always found it at Michigan's Lost Lake Campgrounds.

Randy Bernard has had short stories published in Oakland Community College's Literary Edition, *The Recorder*, as well as written and published a monthly newsletter for the Hope Park Association concerning interests of Old Redford, downstate. A Michigan resident his entire life, currently he lives and writes in Indian River.

After helping pitch the tent, we were anxious to get out on our own. Amy said, "Mom, can Tina and I explore the river bank?" something we did every trip.

"Yes," her mother said, "but wear your life jackets, and don't swim in the river. You know it looks calm on top, but it has a strong current just below the surface. If you want to swim, do it in the lake when you get back."

"Okay!" Amy squealed. We bumped hips in our happy, familiar way. Her face shined with an excitement as bright as the midday sun straight above the pines. "We'll pack some sandwiches, hike to Captain Gordon's old rowboat, eat there, then come back and swim."

"Great," I said.

"Be back before dark so Gordon's ghost doesn't get you," her father called from inside the tent.

"*Daaaaad*," Amy groaned. "We're eleven! We don't believe in ghosts anymore."

"Okay, okay…" her dad said, contrite. "Stick together, the buddy system—and be back before dark. I don't want to come look for you."

Our life vests on, and our lunches tucked inside them, we hiked through the woods to the river's edge. The water was high, over the banks in some places, and our usual dirt trail along side the river was lost below the water somewhere. We allowed ourselves to feel brave as we walked so near a river this dangerous.

Amy spotted a fallen tree which had one large limb that arched across the river for twenty feet, like a bridge built half way. All at once, she darted ahead and danced out to the end of the limb. Her scurry scared off a turtle. It landed in the water with a light *plop*, bobbed on the river's surface a moment, then paddled with all fours to the safety of shore.

"Hey, this is neat," Amy called out as she bounced up and down on the limb, her arms out before her, pretending she was about to dive into the water. "Now for my double somersault, half twist," she announced, as if an Olympic diver, "degree of difficulty two point nine."

"Come back you might fall," I yelled. I pictured her splashing into the river, rapidly swept away by the current, down to the lake, then over Dead Drop Falls.

"Scaredy Cat," she sneered. But slowly, Amy pirouetted her way back along the limb with the grace and balance of a ballerina. It was times like these that I always felt a twinge of jealousy. Not just at her dexterity, but also that so suddenly she could become so carefree. I realized then what a large part that sudden carefree ability was in my liking her. Inside my best friend roamed a spirit more wild than even the woods that surrounded us. And although that self-same, carefree spirit sometimes got us into great trouble, again, I found myself wishing I was her.

"Come on," she said as she jumped from the fallen tree to the ground. "I'll race you to Brontosaurus Rock." She shot off without a second glance to me.

I tore after her. The huge humpback rock was a familiar landmark. We raced a new trail, around trees and through batches of brambles. The sweet smell of their berries burst into the air. The thorny branches picked through my jeans. I barely felt the picks though, because for that moment, while we ran along the river's edge, finally I knew what it was like to be her. *Totally alive.* I imagined us as two wild deer while I continued to run behind her. We ran so long, and hard that I thought I might drop. Thankfully, for my screaming legs, Amy suddenly stopped.

She bent over to get her breath and was holding her side, as if she had a cramp.

When I caught up to her I leaned over to catch my breath, too.

"Got a stitch in your side?" I asked between gulps of air.

"Nuh uh," she said, then stood right up. I saw her try and hide a wince by quickly pointing ahead of us with her arm. "There's Captain Gordon's boat," she said. "We missed Brontosaurus Rock."

I looked back down the river, knowing full well that no one stole it. No one could have lifted it. Because of its size, most of it below ground, its curved top always reminded me of a dinosaur's back. Probably how it got the name, I'd always thought. Then I knew where it was.

"The river covered it," I said. "It's still out there, just underwater."

"Yeah that must be it," she agreed and began walking in the direction of the abandoned rowboat. I fell in step with her, feeling tired, yet somehow, as alive inside as a Fourth of July sparkler. If only everyday could be like this.

We pulled our sack lunches from our vests. After spreading our napkins on the upside down boat, we enjoyed a makeshift picnic. While we ate, we watched a beaver salvaging twigs that rapidly drifted down the river. He clamped one in his mouth after positioning it with his paws, then swam away. A few minutes later he swam back by with his mouth empty, but dark eyes darting each way for another easy castaway.

After a swallow of sandwich, Amy said, "Hey, there's the road we drove in on." She pointed across the river.

I saw a section of dirt road, some hundred feet beyond the far bank. "How do you know that's the same road?" I asked, thinking she wanted to be a know-it-all.

"'Cause I always look to see the rowboat when we come in. You can see it from the car if you look. Except at night, of course…Say," she said, lowering her voice to a whisper, "do you think old Gordon died going over the waterfall?"

"No, Dummy," I said. "If he'd have gone over the falls in his boat like they say, the boat wouldn't be here now. It would have been smashed to bits on the rocks at the bottom of the falls."

"But they say his ghost put it back together, and he still comes back to use it at night. People have seen him."

"Not true," I said.

"It *is*," she said. "They see his cigar glowing in the dark as he glides down the river to the falls in his boat."

"They see fireflies," I said.

She frowned for a moment, and then said, "You're probably right. Adults will make up anything to try and scare us away from the river."

We finished our lunches and put our wrappings back in the bags, to throw away later at the campgrounds. We stuffed them in our life vests. "We'd better get started back," I said. "The sun is already behind the trees. It's going to get dark real fast."

"I wonder if this thing will float?" she asked. I watched her bend over, slide her hands under the lip of the boat where it hit the ground, then lift.

"What are you doing?"

"Come on, help me," she said with a grunt. "We have to turn it over."

She lifted so hard and grunted so loud that I *had* to help her. After all, she was my best friend. We hefted the boat up on

76

its edge then it fell over and away from us in the deep grass. It rocked to a rest.

"Well would you look at that," she said in a sly voice, one I had long since learned meant mischief.

Hoping to deter the wild idea I suspected had taken up residence in her imagination, I decided to play dumb and asked, "Look at what?"

"The *oars* girl! We should have done this before!"

"Come on," I pleaded. "We have to get going. It's late." Already the forest around us was filled with dusky shadow-light.

"If we take the boat we won't even have to row, just steer. The current will take us down to the lake. It's our duty. We'll be conserving energy—our own!" She ran to the pointed bow of the boat and pushed. It moved a few inches toward the water.

"We'll have to test it," I said, and then helped her push. The boat was so old. I just knew it would leak. Once Amy saw that, we could be on our way back, *walking* to the campgrounds.

We wrestled the boat across a strip of tall grass and managed to get the square stern into the river. It floated while I felt the current tugging to take it away. I watched for it to fill with water. I knew it had to leak, since my nose told me the moldy smell that came from within the boat was dry rot, a death sentence to anything that had once floated.

But after several very long minutes, Amy proclaimed, "Dry as a bone! Get in, I'll push us off."

The boat didn't sink. My heart did. There was no stopping her now, and, if I didn't go with her, she'd go it alone. At times like this her middle name was Mule. To make matters worse, I recalled her father telling us: "Stay together, the buddy system." I did not want to get in that boat and onto that river. But I would not desert my best friend.

She tossed the oars in. They *rattled* to rest across the plank board seats. "Get in. I'll push off and turn the nose in the right direction. Isn't this great!"

"No," I said, but climbed in anyway. The tiny boat had three board-beam seats. I sat in the middle. A voice in the back of my mind whispered, *This is absolutely the last stupid thing you will ever do because you are going to drown.* I so hated getting trapped into her schemes. I faced Amy at the front, hoping she could see the daggers in my eyes.

As usual, Amy paid my disapproval no mind. She pushed the boat away from shore, scampering in over the bow at the very last second.

"You're sitting backward," she said with a laugh, as she plopped down next to me on the seat. "We row facing the back."

I turned around to watch her mount her oar in its holder on the side rail of the boat. With dread, I did the same with mine.

"Okay," she said, "we'll row to the middle, then drift."

While we struggled to row to the middle of the river, we drifted quickly, gaining speed with the current. We had easily traveled sixty or seventy feet downstream, yet despite our rowing we were only ten feet from shore—and fifteen feet from the middle. The boat *thudded* into something that jarred us in our seats. We bumped shoulders, while holding our oars to prevent us from toppling backwards over our seats.

"What in the…?" Amy exclaimed.

For a moment we were stopped in the water. Then, slowly the boat worked its way around an obstruction with the push of the current. We looked into the water and caught a glimpse of a large submerged rock.

"There's Brontosaurus Rock," Amy announced, "safe and sound."

"I wish we were 'safe and sound' back at the campgrounds," I said with venom.

"Ninny," she sneered.

Once we had rowed to the center of the river and had the nose of the boat pointed downstream, Amy let her oar rest in the oarlock. The wide end of the oar trailed in the water making a small v-shaped wake. I hung onto my oar for all my life was worth.

If we did make it to the campgrounds, I had half a mind to have her declared officially insane; the other half could declare me insane, too.

We let ourselves drift. Amy marveled: "Look at how tightly the trees line the shore and how the high-up branches on each side curve out and connect over us, like a canopy of green leaves, fitting for a couple of forest queens like us."

Queen's beans, I thought. I saw nothing to marvel at. With the sunlight fading, I felt trapped in an ever-darkening tunnel. "We could row a little more and get back sooner," I said.

If Amy heard me she showed no sign. I followed her now downward glance. Her eyes were fixed on a cigar butt wedged between the seat board and the boat's sidewall. She snatched it up.

"Leave it alone," I said. "It's all yucky with germs."

She brandished it between her first finger and her thumb then pretended to take a puff. Her eyes glistened with a wild look, and she stood bravely up on the seat with one foot on the side rail. The boat rocked dangerously each time she moved, and she seemed to not even notice!

"Ahoy there!" she shouted, one hand proudly on her hip, the other waving the cigar in a wide blustering gesture, "I'm Captain Gordon, and this here's my river! Anyone on it gets grilled for dinner. I have a special hankerin' for innocent young girls."

The stink of the cigar filled my nose, and, for an instant, I pictured a mean old man with a grizzled look and a gray stubble of beard. I imagined a man *so* mean, he would happily grin while watching someone drown. "Sit down; you're scaring me," I told Amy.

She let out a wild laugh and jumped from the seat to the floor of the boat. When she hit, we heard a small *splash*. My heart actually fluttered. We both looked around in shock. The boat was filling with water. It streamed to the back from beneath the last seat and had already pooled in the rear. I turned back around and looked at the floor in the front of the boat. I saw the beginning of the problem. A board must have split when we hit the boulder and widened the nearer it came to the rear. It would be open beneath the back seat.

While we tried to grasp what was happening and what to do, I heard a soft *bump* on the bow and the *screech* of branches along the boat's side. We were drifting beneath the bridge-shaped tree limb that Amy had danced on earlier. As the water pulled us past, a snarl of branches hooked Amy's oar and lifted it.

"Grab it!" I yelled.

"My paddle!" Amy screamed. She reached for it and missed. The current carried us away before she could try again. We watched, intense with fear, as for a moment, the oar stood upright in the water with the handle end caught in the tree. In the very next instant, the current sucked the oar down, completely out of sight.

"Did you see that?" Amy asked quietly.

I watched for the oar to bob back up. It never did.

"Let's get to shore," I said.

"Let's," she agreed, still staring where the oar had gone under. "It was like a hand grabbed it and yanked it right down," she said, turning to look at me. Her eyes were wide. She didn't need to say whose hand she had been thinking of.

"See, I told you this was a stupid idea," I said.

"You did not," she shot right back.

I clenched my teeth and pulled my oar as hard as I could, hoping to get us from the middle of the river back to the bank. Without a word Amy grabbed the oar too. We both pulled as hard as we could.

After several minutes, we were out of energy. All we had accomplished was spinning ourselves in circles in the middle of the river.

"I guess I really did it this time," she said.

A quiver in her voice made me more alarmed. It was the first time I'd ever heard her truly frightened. "Better start bailing," I said.

"Bail with what?"

"Your hands, your shoes, *anything*, or we'll sink. I'll keep trying to steer us over to the edge." When I looked over to get my bearings, the bank seemed to blend with the woods. Everything was shadow. As I tried to come up with a plan, I realized that by the time we drifted to the lake, full darkness would have fallen. Maybe the current would be less at the lake, and we could make a swim for shore there. I could only hope.

"Oh, this isn't going to work," Amy cried out. Her voice had the high pitch of panic. She bailed with her cupped hands, yet the boat continued to fill with water…first an inch, then two inches of water, and then three….

"It's no good," I said, now feeling the cold water climb my ankles. The boat began to tilt to one side. "We have to swim to shore," I said. As I looked around, I saw that we had already drifted into the lake. While it wasn't pitch dark, a fog was rising, and I couldn't see our campgrounds or the direction of the waterfall. We would have to swim, but if we lost our way, we might just swim right over the falls.

"Do you hear that?" Amy asked.

I heard a low *rumbling*.

"Yeah," I said. "It might be thunder, a ways away though."

Amy quit bailing and hurried to sit by me. She grabbed hold of my upper arm with both of her hands and squeezed. "That's not thunder," she quietly said looking into the fog and darkness. "That's the sound of Dead Drop Falls." Her voice was barely a whisper. "The current is going to take us straight to the waterfall and over the edge. What are we going to do?"

"If we're headed to the falls, we'll just swim the other way," I said, pointing past her on her side of the boat, away from the rumble. "This lake's not all that big. We'll have to hit shore somewhere."

I dropped my oar across the seat top. I looked all around, trying to pinpoint the direction of the falls by their sound. In the one direction it seemed louder. I strained my ears and eyes.

Through the fog I saw a faint red pulsing light. It brightened, then dimmed, brightened, then dimmed.

"What are you staring at?" Amy asked, but when she saw the tiny red glow, she answered herself, "It's him," she whispered right in my ear. In a small shaky voice she added, "That's the glow of his cigar."

We held each other's hands. It couldn't be Gordon's cigar as he puffed on it, I thought. There were no such things as ghosts. "Fireflies," I said, trying to sound brave.

"His ghost wants the boat back," Amy said as if not hearing me. "Or he wants us to go over the falls and crash and be killed just like him."

"Take off your shoes," I ordered. I broke her grip on my arm as I kicked my shoes off.

"Why?" she asked, but her voice sounded empty and far away. I didn't think she was really thinking. When I looked right at her, she seemed hypnotized by the pulsing red light.

"Come on," I yelled. I bent down and felt for one of her feet below the water in the boat and pulled off her sneaker. I did the same for the other one. "We're going to swim for it."

She looked at me. I could barely see her in the darkness and fog, but her eyes were definitely saying, *No*.

"We have life vests; we'll stay on the surface. We can swim for shore. I'll race you!" I challenged, hoping to snap her out of it.

"I can't," she said. "I'm too scared." Again both her hands latched onto my one upper arm.

"I'm scared too," I said. I struggled to get up in the tilting boat, pulling her to her feet with me. "We'll stand on the seat, do belly smackers so we stay above the water, and then we'll swim."

"I'll get a cramp," she complained. "I had one earlier from running. I won't be able to make it. Don't leave me," she begged. I saw a single tear slip from the corner of her eye. I didn't know which frightened me more: a ghost, us going over the falls, or my best and bravest friend crumbling right before me. If I let myself get as frightened as her, I knew we'd never make it. All the while, the once low rumble of Dead Drop Falls was now becoming a *roar*.

"Put your arm around my waist," I said, forcing her to change her hold on me. "Look over here, the way we're going to go." She didn't. I had to turn her head away from the red glow with both my hands, nearly losing my balance in the process. "Take a deep breath," I ordered.

"Wait," she screamed. She looked up into the enshrouding fog. "Please, God, don't let me drown," she said.

"Ditto," I said, and took one last look behind us before we jumped. Fear made me freeze. In the fog, as if standing on the water, was a man dressed in black. His beard was gray, his face wrinkled with age. A cigar glowed at the corner of his mouth, "Ya better get goin' now if yer gonna be gettin' at all," he warned with a crooked grin.

"What did you say?" Amy asked. From the corner of my eye, I could see her begin to turn toward me.

I screamed, "Jump!" then grabbed her and took her over the side with me. We splashed face first into the dark, dangerous water.

Immediately it consumed us. I felt cold water up my nose. Water filled my ears. I knew we would drown. But then we bobbed right back up. I heard Amy gagging for air in a panic. "Swim!" I screamed. "Swim!"

"Don't leave me!" she yelled and struggled to hold onto me.

"Swim, stay close, we'll keep talking." I forced her hands off me and slipped underwater in the process. I came up and spit a mouthful of water like a city fountain. I pushed her in front of me, yelling, "Swim, swim." Her arms started to splash. "That's a girl," I said, "Left arm, right arm," I ordered and dog paddled behind her. I gave her a light, lifting push every other stroke.

Then we heard an eerie deep voice from everywhere in the fog calling: "*Aaaammyy… Tiiinnaaaa…*"

"He knows our names. He's after us!" Amy cried out and stopped trying to swim.

"Just block it out," I yelled. I grabbed the shoulder of her life vest and began kicking my legs with all my strength, pulling her along, "Come on, you can do it," I said between gulps for air. I knew she could. But I would pull her to shore if I had to.

Soon I could feel she was kicking because she became easier to tow. In another moment she was doing fine on her own. I was afraid to look back to see if the pulsing red light was gaining on us, but our names kept getting called louder and louder.

"God, don't let old Gordon get us," Amy sobbed as she swam. "If you let us live, we'll never take another boat—or anything—ever!"

After what seemed like hours, my strength nearly gone, it felt like a supernatural event when my toes kicked sandy lake bottom sending a sharp pain up my leg and into my hip. We could stand. We hurried onto the shore. I quickly looked back and couldn't see the red light. "He's gone!" I shouted.

Then a voice, not far from us in the dark called, "Amy? Tina? Is that you?" We grabbed onto each other, frightened all over again. We shook and shivered.

"W-who's there?" I asked.

A flashlight beam blinded my eyes.

"It's me, girls."

"Dad!" Amy screamed in relief.

We raced to the light.

Amy hugged him.

"Hold on, hold on. Are you two all right?"

"We are now," I said.

Amy began to cry. "He was after us, Dad!"

Her father looked from her to me, his face questioning, then his eyes darted to the darkness for any lurking danger. He frowned while shining his flashlight around. "Who?" he asked, as he continued to look for someone.

"The ghost," Amy blurted out. "We took his boat, and he came after us."

Continuing to shine his light among the trees near shore, Amy's dad listened while she told him everything.

As I listened, I did not know if I had seen the ghost or not. Maybe it was panic, I reasoned. But he had seemed so real!

Amy finished her story, "…after we saw his cigar, we had to jump for the water… I wouldn't have made it without Tina, Dad. She saved my life."

I saw a flood of kindness and warmth filling her father's eyes as he looked down on me. He gently pulled me to him and embraced me with one, large arm. Amy was still in his other arm.

After a moment, her father replied to her story. All he said was, "I see."

From the sound of his voice I knew the stern adult was back. "If you two aren't hurt, I guess I'd better take you to your ghost."

I cringed.

"What?" Amy cried.

"It's all right," he said. "It's not really a ghost. You just thought it was."

We followed him and his flashlight beam down the trail at the edge of the lake.

"There's your ghost," he said and we watched the circle of light as he pointed it out through the fog on the lake. Out about fifty feet before the falls was a floating buoy marker with a pulsing red light at the top. "You know there's no swimming at this end of the lake. The light is to warn away boats at night."

I looked at the red light, then tried to recall the face I had seen in the fog. Could fear have made me imagine it? I suppose it must have, and tried to make myself believe it was so.

Just as we were turning to leave the falls, the flashlight picked up something else in the water.

"The boat, that's it there, Dad," Amy cried out. Just the triangle of the bow was above the waterline, like a shark's nose, as the boat drifted steadily toward the edge of the falls. Over it went. We barely heard it *crash* on the rocks at the bottom through the *roar* of the waterfall. Amy leaned closer to me and whispered in my ear, "That could have been us."

"Yeah," I deadpanned, "some adventure." I noticed her dad heard us, and I thought he was going to lecture us.

But all he said was, "Let's get going back to camp. We'll talk later." We all took one last look to the bottom of the falls. We saw broken sections of boat drifting downstream. It was totally destroyed.

Back at camp, we snuggled up safely in our sleeping bags, absolutely exhausted. I found myself missing my home and my family. Just as I was drifting off to sleep, I thought I heard Amy whisper, "I wish I was you. You always know the right things to do. I'm going to listen to you more often. You're my very best friend."

The next day, we took down the tent and policed our campsite for litter. No one mentioned the boat trip or waterfall. I had wanted to ask Amy if I had really heard her say something last night. But the idea struck me as dumb. *Her* wanting to be like *me*? It was easier to believe I'd seen a ghost.

Later, as we drove along the old camp road on our way out, I wondered, again, maybe for the hundredth time that day: How had I imagined a face in the fog—a ghost that seemed so real? At that very moment, Amy clasped my hand on the car seat and squeezed. I looked over to where I thought she was looking. Then I understood. Upside down on the bank and all in one piece was Captain Gordon's old rowboat.

Everfaithful

Veronica Anne Starbuck

He lay silently in the hospital bed they'd fixed for him in the spare bedroom, because he'd gotten too weak to take the stairs.

Awakening, he breathed in deeply the cool spring air that blew in fresh and clean through the open window, and he watched the snowy-white curtains flutter and move in the wind. The green smell of grass and trees and earth lingered in the air, refreshing, and it filled his tired lungs with the promise of springtime, and It stirred almost-forgotten memories of a boyhood long since used up. With the unbearable sweetness of the day dancing in his senses, the freshness broke loose a flood of memories: all the springs that had slipped past him, whispers on a warm wind he'd

Veronica Anne Starbuck resides in Michigan with her husband, young daughter, and three Basenji dogs. She has an MA in English from Oakland University. Her first novel, *August Magic*, is ASPCA approved and was recently nominated for a Maxwell Medallion by the Dog Writer's Association of America.

ridden blissfully--until one October morning had sent him crashing headlong into the reality that he was no longer a child, but a fifty-two year old man who had cancer and was going to die.

Sometimes, the shock of it frightened him, but lately, as the days grew longer and the chill of winter retreated, a quietness settled upon him, easing the fears and tempering the reality. After all he'd been through, and after his long fight, he discovered a tiredness that simply wouldn't go away. All the sleep in the world didn't help; all the time spent in bed instead of on the sofa in the living room or on the front porch steps couldn't quite take the edge off the fatigue; it was as much a part of him as the air he breathed. And oh, how sweet the spring air was.

In bygone days, he'd often lie in bed on spring mornings, listening to his wife move through the house, and pretend he was still a young man, or even still, a little boy. What a joy it was to convince himself that the only thought in his mind was to spring out of bed, have breakfast and see what treasures the day held. Perhaps there would be June strawberries, a baseball game down at the corner sandlot, or a tree to climb. Try as he might, though, in his illness he found he was unable to duplicate the dream, it had eluded him, escaping with his health and future in the blink of an eye. Now he was, to use a well-worn phrase, merely a shadow of his former self, pale and thin, with dark circles under his blue-gray eyes, a stubble of a beard growing on his face and chin. *Never mind the shaving,* he'd told his wife, suddenly deciding one rainy morning a week ago. It no longer mattered. *Never mind it, anyway. They'll shave me when the time comes.*

And suddenly, his room was aglow with rosy-golden late afternoon sunlight, and it was the sunlight that danced against the window glass, casting shadows about the room: tall shadows near the window where the flowers were, shorter ones where the dusty bookcase full of well-read, well-worn books leaned up against the wall, and on his bed a small, dark, dog-shaped shadow that was his little tricolored Basenji dog, Star.

She lay in a patch of sunlight that fell across the soft blanket on his bed, curled into a warm little ball with ears that twitched at his slightest movement, gazing at him through the dark, liquid eyes when he raised a hand and let it rest gently on the curve of her back. From delicate white paws she raised her head, breathed deeply, and began to lick his hand with her little pink tongue. The sensation was a pleasant one, bringing instant warmth to his fingers and palm.

Star herself was an older dog, and the years had been kind to her as she'd run and jumped and played her way through them, slowing her down as they will with all dogs, but as they will with Basenjis, aging her as gracefully as they would allow. She had never done well in the show ring, although his daughter had placed high hopes on her and had spent quite a large amount of money toward that end. Nonetheless, he always believed fate had brought Star to his doorstep, and easily looked past his daughter's disappointment in the pretty little tricolor who'd been a failure as a show dog, but who'd become a second shadow to himself, a real champion to the cause of making sure he never had to be alone.

Star had taken to him at once, and it wasn't long before he, too, was smitten. He'd always admired his daughter's Basenjis, those African barkless dogs with the worry-wrinkled faces and tightly-curled tails. He loved the feel of their short silky coats, loved the clean, dry-grass smell of them, and found endless amusement in their kitten-like antics. Who would have thought that a nearly mute dog that cleaned itself like a cat would work her way into his heart? Star knew it could be so, and from the moment they met, she was in love.

Whenever he'd look up, she'd be somewhere nearby, curled up into a little ball on the old green-plaid sofa in the garage when he was working on a car; laying belly down, frog-dog style in the cool grass as he mowed the lawn on summer afternoons; or stretched out across his bare toes as he shaved in the morning before leaving her at the front door and heading off to work. She would have followed him if she could, he knew, and once in a while when he had to work a Saturday, she'd accompany him to the office, playing with papers from the waste cans, and acting as if the world was merely there to greet and fawn over her.

She had plenty of admirers, Star did, and was every bit a lady to anyone who wanted to stop and pet the little masked dog with the triple-curled tail that followed her master on long walks through the neighborhood. Star didn't have a mean hair on her compact little body. She liked all she met with equal measure, but there was only one person she loved, and she made no bones about it, either. Star was his dog, his bright and shining lady, completely, wholly, and unfailingly.

Of late Star's eyes had failed her, and he'd made it a point of asking his wife not to move furniture, for if it wasn't exactly where Star had remembered it, she'd walk into it. However attentive and well meaning his wife was, she would sometimes forget. Always dignified, Star would let out a small distressed yelp when she stumbled over something or walked into it, but she always recovered with the unique dignity that was a hallmark of her Basenji nature. Then she'd carefully sniff and circle the object until she knew exactly what it was, and where it was.

Right from the start, his illness had troubled the little Basenji. Gone were the long walks in the autumn sun she'd come to expect. As the leaves fell from the trees, he wasn't out in the yard raking the red and gold into large piles for her to dive into and hide in. He tried to explain to her what was going on, and she'd prick her dark little ears and tilt her head to one side as he talked. Her brow would wrinkle even more with concentration as she tried to make her Basenji mind understand his words. She couldn't, of course, but the serious tone in his voice made her sit up and take notice, and she knew that something was terribly wrong.

It broke her heart to be left alone in the house when he had to stay in the hospital for long periods of time. Her brow furrowed, anxious and wondering where he'd been and what he'd been doing; she'd sniff him for hours when he'd finally return. He'd missed her dreadfully then, his little shadow dog who'd always been there, who desperately wanted to be, but wasn't allowed to be. If he needed his little shadow before, he needed her more than ever now.

She, too, was lost without her shadow, for she'd come to depend on him to be there when darkness had taken the light from her eyes. They were two of a kind, the little old Basenji and the not-so-old-but-very-ill man. Each needed the other, and each was lost without the other.

He stroked her dark coat gently, marveling at the softness of it beneath his thin hand. She continued to lick his other hand, and it was comforting to him.

Everfaithful.

The word crept into his mind, unbidden, the way memories will if given proper invitation. He began to think about the times they'd shared — how she'd sit next to him when he'd drive up the dusty road into town for a newspaper, and how they'd secretly shared ice cream cones on humid August afternoons. He remembered the time she'd met a skunk, and endured the indignity of tomato juice baths until the scent of it was barely perceptible. He remembered how she'd pounced on a garter snake and killed it in the grass when he was cutting the lawn. It was not so dangerous a snake, but nevertheless, a threat to her beloved. She'd been so proud of that snake, he remembered with a small smile. And then there was that time when he'd been out shoveling snow, and she'd been there with him, chasing snowballs, sometimes catching them in her mouth. He remembered how, when he'd fallen on the ice and knocked the wind out of himself, she'd hovered over him, licking his face until he could breathe properly again.

Everfaithful.

He watched as she stopped licking his hand, stood up on the bed, and stretched, letting her tail unfurl and reaching rearward with first one leg, then the other, toes flexing and curling. She leaned forward and stretched some more, and when she was satisfied, she gave herself a shake that made the bed move. She stood unsteadily for a moment, the late afternoon glow upon her dark shoulders and back like a warm cloak. He called her name, once, in a low tone. At the sound of his voice she turned her head toward him and took a few gentle steps until she could settle her paws even more gently on his chest. Gentler still, she lay her masked head on her paws, and sighed.

Her breath was a caress, a little flutter, on his cheek.

The sunlight was still on her, and he studied the features of her face, noticing how the short, fine, red hairs grew along her muzzle, how the tiny patch of pink skin above her nose grew pinker in the heat of the sun, and how the fine pencil-width line of white hairs traced their way through ebony ones to the little white diamond star between her rust-colored pips, the star that inspired her name. He whispered her name several more times, and watched as her ears moved toward the sound of his voice. He smelled the sweet, warm grass-like smell that was she, and he softly traced the star pattern on her brow with his finger.

"Do you remember," he began, "the morning you came to live here?"

She lifted her head from his chest, turning it to one side. *Yes,* her face said, *tell me that story again.*

In a quiet voice he began to talk to her, reminding them both of the history that they shared, and of the good times, as well as the bad ones.

There were summers on the lake where they'd get up before dawn and creep down to the landing to watch the sunrise; afternoons where she'd sleep in his canoe, soaking up the sunlight while he fished for trout. There were trick-or-treaters at Halloween, greeted at the door by a little, curly-tailed dog that wore her own dark mask year-round, and looked beautiful in it. Together, they had traveled through the neighborhood, across side roads, back roads, and interstates, remembering the squirrels and cats they'd met along the way, recounting countless cool melting treats from the ice cream truck, remembering birthdays and Christmases, and an entire lifetime they'd shared.

As they reminisced, the afternoon wore on, and time stood respectively still, patiently waiting. Then, as all good stories must, the end came on tiptoes and paw pads, quiet, silent. A gentle breeze warmed the cold room and carried them together out of his tiredness and her darkness, rising through crimson cloud tops into a brightness that was dazzling; there sunlight played in eternal summertime and youth; and there a young boy ran through tall grass with a dainty sprite of a tricolor Basenji bounding joyfully after him.

And when the sun had set and the last warm rays had faded the sky from rose to purple to a crystal blue, the shadows that had lingered on the walls and behind bookcases crept from their places and filled the emptiness of the room, stardust lingering in the moonlit panes of an open window. White curtains, illuminated by ghostly-pale blue moonlight fluttered and moved in the wind. The smell of grass and trees and earth lingered in the air, refreshing, filling the room where two had once been, whispering in the darkness.

Everfaithful.

Boundaries: Lance's Story

Chris F. Hauge

Stone Throw Cottage, Windermere Point…Mackinac Island, Michigan

Sitting at one of the worn dew-dampened picnic tables closest to the water, I imagine all the times Betsy, my patient, sat here on this point of land, enjoying the air, even as I breathe in the fresh early morning lake smells. Looking past the Round Island lighthouse, I lose myself in the first sunrise I have experienced on Mackinac Island since my arrival yesterday. The colors are now crimson, melting into gold against an otherwise cloudless, emerald blue ski. It is bittersweet, this morning, to be able to see, hear, smell, taste and feel Mackinac Island for myself. I realize I will no longer experience all of this through Betsy's senses:

> **Dr. Chris F. Hauge** has history with *Voices of Michigan,* having served as a reader for nonfiction for Volume I. His story *Stone Throw Cottage: Betsy's Story* was published in Volume II. Chris and his wife, Sally, live in Wilmington, NC, where Chris is a psychotherapist and university professor.

she had so lovingly described her island in my therapy sessions with her. I wonder at Betsy's dying wisdom, which sent me on this final mission to her island to live in her Stone Throw Cottage.

Cherry Tree Farm, Hannington…Wick, England

I have known a young boy inside my head as far back as I can remember. My name is actually Peter Lance, the name my mother used to call me, when I was in trouble. I always preferred to use only Lance. So, since childhood I have called the boy in my head, Peter. I suppose Lance is my outer self, and Peter is my private self. Peter has always been eleven years old, and came to stay with me before the time I started school. Even when I was four or five years old, I knew that somehow, my friend Peter was much more than the imaginary playmate many children invent to fill in the empty, dull-gray, ever-present ache that we later learned to label as loneliness. Much later, as I was learning about, and then actually treating patients with multiple personalities, I saw Peter as my protector alter ego. Still, I knew he was more than an imaginary brother, playmate, or even protector. In spite of the fact that he never grew older than eleven, I have always known him as a very wise, old soul, within me.

This was confirmed, when, during one of our early therapy sessions, my patient, Betsy, described driving down a country road in the Cotswolds of England with her English friend, Trevor.

"We had just left a little village called Kempsford, and were looking for the headwaters of the River Thames. We were on an open stretch of road with lush green fields, stone fences, and deep ditches on either side. Trevor was describing how the stone fences were built with field stones carefully selected and fitted, one on top of the other, with such care and skill, that no mortar was necessary; and they have stood for centuries. As we came to a bridge crossing the Thames, Trevor stopped the car, and we got out to stand on the bridge. Trevor pointed to a two-story building on our left with weather-beaten stone walls the color of the golden sunlight shining on them. He proudly told me that this cottage was appropriately named Bridge Farm. It has been there for the five hundred years during which a bridge has crossed the Thames at that location."

Listening to Betsy's story, I stopped breathing for a moment. I knew exactly where Betsy was in England. I had been at that exact place, myself, many times. In fact, I knew the English couple who lived at Bridge Farm. I felt a cold shudder down my spine as the tiny hairs on the back of my neck came to attention. The shudder and hair are always a sign that I am touching something very private that crosses the imaginary boundaries separating my experience from my patients'.

Betsy's eyes were wide and glistening blue with the wonder of what she was sharing with me. "Trevor suggested that we leave the car and walk. As we walked, and I felt the crunch of tiny rocks beneath me, I saw a boy with sturdy boots on. I knew I had walked this road before, and I was so happy and comfortable. Is that strange, Doc?"

Betsy gazed intently on my face. I knew she was looking for any sign of disbelief before she would continue sharing this very real, very private, experience with me. She had nothing to fear. It was as if I was there with her, because I had many times walked that same road in the Cotswolds of England. I spent a year there studying Social Work at Oxford after leaving Viet Nam and the Air Force in 1966.

I assured her, "What you experienced is not strange at all, Betsy. Go on. I'm with you." I didn't tell her how much we were at one.

Betsy hardly heard my assurances, as she eagerly continued. "I took Trevor's hand as we walked by Yew Tree Farm, Sycamore Tree Farm, and Manor Farm. He told me that the village of Hannington Wick, with its series of farms and farmhouses, had changed little since the Manor was acquired by Sir Thomas Freke in 1605."

Betsy was on the edge of her chair with excitement. I knew what she was about to say. "Doc, after Manor Farm, we came to the most beautiful three-story stone house. The sun was just beginning to set, giving the stones a golden hue against a purple-and-rose sky backdrop. We came up to the gate, and on a weather-beaten oak sign was the name--"

"Cherry Tree Farm," I quietly finished Betsy's sentence.

Betsy came to her feet as though she had been hit with a jolt of electricity from a cattle prod. "How, how did you know that, Doc?"

I knew only that I was having as much trouble understanding what was happening to us, as was Betsy. "Betsy, I lived at Cherry Tree Farm for a year in 1966 while I was studying at Oxford."

Betsy slumped back into her chair, her mouth agape. "You lived at Cherry Tree Farm? I can't believe it!"

I suppose I had to prove something to her, or maybe I just wanted to share my excitement over the experience we had both shared. In any case, I took her hands, and looked directly into her deep blue eyes. "You can believe it, Betsy. As you stood at the gate, the small wall with the sign on it was to your left, wasn't it?" Betsy nodded as I continued with my proof. "There was a row of cherry trees in front of the twelve-paned windows of the great room. On the second floor, you were looking at the master bedroom where I slept. To the right, you saw a weather-beaten door leading into the kitchen, where the original huge cooking fireplace still stands." My words rushed with no thought as to what was coming next, as I relived, in a few sentences, the whole year that I spent in England. "To the right of that, you were looking at the attached building that still has the original cooking fireplace from the fourteenth century, when Cherry Tree Farm was built. The roof was gray, broken slate, wasn't it?"

Betsy was finally able to respond, tears forming in her eyes. "Yes, with three chimneys. I can't believe this. What's happening?"

I wasn't sure that I had any more answers than she, but I wanted to let Betsy know that we had the same experience, eighteen years apart. So, I went on. "When I was first shown Cherry Tree Farm by the British couple who lived at Bridge Farm, it was late October, at sunset, just like you first saw it." I found myself becoming even more intent and excited. "I knew that I had been there before, just like you knew you had walked that road before. When I went inside, I instantly experienced the most intense peace and comfort. It was like coming home after a long, long time."

Betsy interrupted me with her own excitement. "Yes, I saw that young boy for some reason. But it was so comfortable, as though there was no time at all, just…now."

As a rainstorm blew in from the ocean, Betsy and I spent the rest of that night, and into the early morning, in my office, just sharing the experience of Cherry Tree Farm. The storm was one of those Atlantic coastline storms that begins with rain drops the size of Kennedy half dollars. The rain drops become so many that they gradually turn into a silver sheet that seems to hang perpendicular in the wind, occasionally split by pencil-thin rapiers of lightning.

We were no longer dying patient and therapist. We were just old friends reliving a shared experience, from years past.

As the storm intensified, and then waned into dawn, I told Betsy of the story of the Ghost of Hannington Wick, who, allegedly, wandered from farm to farm. I told her about Regan and Charles, my British neighbors who lived at Bridge Farm. Charles was an officer in the English Rangers, and often, when he was in the field, Regan took me around the English countryside she had known since childhood, and recounted her extensive knowledge of the history of the area.

Regan was the first person I ever told of Peter, after she shared her belief in guides who ease our transitions from life to life on earth.

As the night and the storm progressed toward dawn, Betsy talked openly of her return to the United States; her struggle with AIDS; and choosing to confront her own death, on her own terms, without drugs. She wanted me to have Stone Throw Cottage after she died, and told me why it was important to her that I make the trip to Mackinac Island: She wanted me to scatter her ashes among the Lake Huron stones in front of her beloved Stone Throw Cottage.

We decided that the next day we would use hypnosis to further explore the Cherry Tree Farm experience.

Peter's Story…
The next day was Betsy's age regression session. Through hypnosis, this day, she would become twenty-six years old, again. This age regression was nothing new for Betsy. She had become experienced in moving rapidly from eye closure, to the levitation of her left arm, and into deep trance.

I took her back to the road in Hannington Wick. I asked her to observe as the twenty-six year old.

In trance, her voice was quiet, but sure. "I am watching the eleven-year old boy I saw when I was with Trevor. He has on a tweed cap, a sweater with a shirt underneath, a pair of wool tweed pants to the knees, and stockings down to black, ankle-high shoes, with thick soles."

Again I felt the cold up and down my spine and hairs on my neck. Betsy was describing the Peter I had known in my head since childhood, right down to how I saw him dressed.

"He's carrying a snow white goose over his shoulder. I think it's early in the morning, because there is fog rising from the Thames river. Peter turns his head and smiles. As I catch up to him, he tells me that it is his responsibility to keep the birds in the field behind Cherry Tree Farm, where he lives. I tell him who I am, and why I am here, right now. His eyes shine as he says he already knows why I am here.   Even though he is much younger, I somehow don't need to question his wisdom."

Betsy was in deep trance, but her face vividly expressed her feelings. "Peter has black hair, large blue eyes, and very fair skin. He must get little or no sun, and his very pale face accentuates really red lips. I get the feeling his skin is pale because he is very sick. It is very hard for him to breathe, and he coughs a lot, until he's just not able to breathe anymore. I think he is going to die soon."

Betsy nearly lifted out of the chair in horror. "Oh my God! I can see him in a small box on sawhorses in an ancient stone church. Doc, I know he's going to die soon."

In tears she settled back into the chair. "He says he has to go. He walks up the path through the cherry trees, and into the kitchen door of Cherry Tree Farm. Somehow, I can see his mother is very sad, but Peter tells her that it's all right."

Betsy's closed eyes continued to spill over with tears, as she paused and then, whispered, "Christ, Peter drowns himself in the Thames River, rather than die slowly of tuberculosis."

I asked Betsy if she knew the date. "It's like Halloween night. I think it's 1932. I can see jack-o-lanterns and witches in bound stalks of corn. He killed himself at the bridge just up the road from Cherry Tree Farm on Halloween, 1932."

As I slowly brought Betsy back, she left Cherry Tree Farm. Instead of returning to my office, however, she detoured, in her mind, to the steps of Stone Throw Cottage on Mackinac Island. *Her* spiritual core, Elizabeth, was there. Elizabeth took Betsy's hand and walked her to the front door of the cottage.

As Betsy awakened, returning to my office, we were both crying.

Now I knew that Peter was not simply some imaginary playmate. Peter Wood died on October 31, 1932, and I was born on October 31st, ten years later. The Peter with me since childhood was my soul, in my past life as Peter Wood, and is my soul, my spiritual guide, in this life.

Sarah Elizabeth…

I began the age regression in Betsy's next session by asking Betsy to go back to her birth on December 31, 1968, and then back before she was born, to 1964.

At that point, her hand rose to signal me to stop. "I can see a little girl in her front yard. She has a dress on that comes to her knees. She's four or five years old with curly, light brown hair. She's thumping around in circles in the yard and laughing. I can see that there is a row of cars parked in the driveway and on the street. I know she's not supposed to, but she runs into the street."

Betsy paused here: "Oh, there's a car coming! It hits the little girl, hard. She flies through the air to land by a large tree."

Betsy was crying openly. "The man who was driving rushes to her and is holding her. Her head is bleeding, and she's bleeding from her ears. She's crying because she knows she wasn't supposed to go into the street. Now she's coughing up blood and is very frightened. She doesn't understand what's happening to her.

"The man is yelling for help as her mother comes out of the house. She's holding the little girl and rocking back and forth. The girl is saying, 'I'm very sorry…I'm very sorry,' over and over again.

"Then she is quiet, and I can see her lift out of herself, and she seems to pick *me* up out of *my* chair here. Now we're both in the air looking down at her mother holding her. The little girl smiles and tells me that she's glad it's over, because it really hurt. Now she doesn't hurt anymore, but she is sad to leave her mother.

"Her mother is crying and saying, 'Sarah, Sarah. No! No, please no!' It seems like someone is calling Sarah's name from behind us."

There was a long pause before Betsy continued. "I turn around with Sarah, and it's dark; only it's not dark. I can move without moving my body. Everything seems very calm. There are other people all around, further ahead. I can't see them, but I know they are there."

There was another long pause. "It's very peaceful, and I begin to see shadows of people. The shadows take Sarah from me by opening my hand holding her, even though I don't want to let her go. Sarah separates from me and goes with them. They are all like light: so many lights that it makes the darkness turn to gray, and then pure white, and then the white wraps around Sarah. One shadow comes up and says that it's very sorry, but I cannot come with Sarah right now. The shadow goes off to the light, and becomes smaller and smaller, until just a dot of light, and then disappears. Now it's just me, and it's black, and not as warm."

Betsy smiled with her eyes still closed. "I'm now back on the steps of my parent's home, Stone Throw Cottage, on Mackinac Island. I loved to spend summers there. There's a little girl beside me. It's me at five years old. She says her name is Elizabeth. She looks just like Sarah. She's so beautiful."

I instructed Betsy in self-hyphosis so she could explore between sessions.

Walls…

Betsy returned to the next therapy session eager to share her first experience with self-hypnosis. "When I put myself into trance, I came out of the front door of Stone Throw Cottage, and Elizabeth was waiting for me on the front steps. Elizabeth said that if I walked from the steps toward the gate, I would meet Peter again. As I stepped from the last step, and opened the gate, Peter was there, but there were no hedgerows, and we weren't in England. Peter laughed, and told me, 'That's right. You're not in England. You're near Edinborough, Scotland.' He took off his hat, and put his arm around me. I no longer heard his efforts to breathe, and he looked like a healthy eleven-year old boy.

"Peter took me to a very high stone wall stretching as far as I could see. He pointed to it, and told me that this was my wall. He said that once I cross to the other side there will be many others. I asked him how I would ever get over the wall. He smiled again, and said quietly, that I would lift up, and would simply go to the wall.

"I didn't see how I would ever be able to do that. Again, he repeated quietly, but with certainty in his voice, that I would go over the wall. I just couldn't try, or force myself, he said. He affirmed that when the time is right I will do what I have to do.

"I had the sense that I was to go *through* the wall, not over it, or around it. I told him that I didn't think I could get through it right now. Again he smiled, and his blue eyes sparkled, as he repeated that I would be able to do what I needed to, in time.

"Peter suggested that we walk back down the road. The air was cold and damp, the kind of cold and damp that makes your nose and cheeks turn red. I was having some trouble breathing, but not Peter. I asked him how he got the name Peter. He proudly told me how his mother had named him after Saint Peter. He had always thought those were pretty big shoes to fill, but he loved the name.

"Then we were back at the gate to Cherry Tree Farm. Peter squatted down in the road, picked up a small rock, and looked up at me as he turned the rock over in his hand. He told me that just as this small stone in the road is a part of this infinitely longer road stretching in either direction, each of our lives are but a tiny part of the grand plan God has for our souls.

"With that, Peter stood and smiled, and I brought myself back to the porch of Stone Throw Cottage and then up to fully awake."

The Meeting...

This morning sitting at Windermere Point, I am able to see my own spiritual core, Peter, play with Betsy's spiritual core, Elizabeth, for the first time. Betsy, my dear love, is now dead. Elizabeth is dressed in dark blue overhauls, with huge yellow daises splattered indiscriminately over them, just as Betsy described her. Under the overhauls, a white turtleneck hugs her tiny throat partially covered by curly long brown hair. Peter is as I had always pictured him, and as Betsy saw him, when she was on the road passing Cherry Tree Farm. He is running and breathing easily.

The Metamorphosis...

Will I ever be able to share with someone else the joy of sitting in the early Michigan morning sun watching these two children, these two very old souls, playing and laughing together while they skip stones into Lake Huron from Windermere Point? No one else on Mackinac Island can see anything but a graying man sitting alone at a picnic table, smiling to himself, and looking toward the sun rising over the Straits of Mackinac.

Softened by a fresh street washing in progress on Lakeshore Road, the fresh smell of horse manure, "street fudge," brings me back to the cool warmth of the early morning sun now drying the tears on my face. Lakeshore Road is still devoid of the clip clop of the horses. The street cleaners are at their work, and a few shop owners come out to prepare for the day.

I have scattered Betsy's ashes on the stones in front of Stone Throw Cottage and have thrown her urn as far as I could into Lake Huron.

With this release of the pain of my grief, I am now able to see Elizabeth for the first time, in my own mind, with Peter. Letting go of Betsy takes me through one of *my* walls to another level of understanding. Death has finally split open my protective cocoon, forcing me to go inside for my own answers.

Perhaps each of us is facing our own wall of guilt, anger, resentment and our fear of letting go. To get through that wall, we must simply let go. On the other side of the wall is the joy of collectiveness and completion with soulmates.

I'm not sure how long I will have Elizabeth to visit with, but I have come out of my protective cocoon, and can now fly as a full-grown monarch butterfly, on my own.

Voices of Michigan

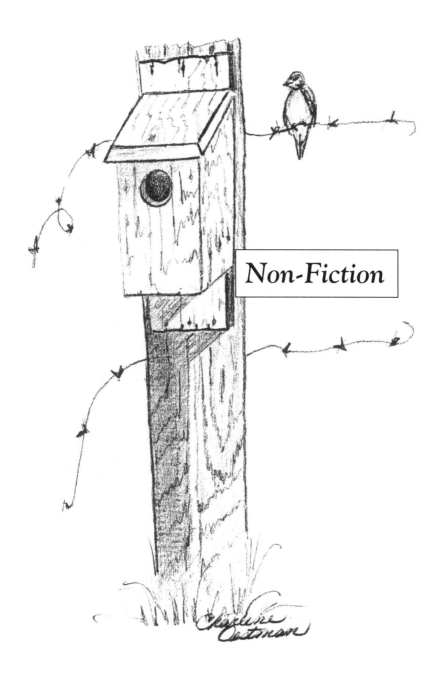

Non-Fiction

Thanks,
Mike VanBuren

Twilight Limited

Mike VanBuren

The world outside is dark, and I'm sitting in the brightly lit dining car of Amtrak's *Twilight Limited*. The train is rolling east along steel rails that stretch from Union Station in Chicago to the small, red-stone depot in Kalamazoo -- and beyond.

I lean forward and place my elbows on the narrow table in front of me. I hear the powerful rumble of the diesel locomotive that is pulling me through the cold southwestern Michigan night. Its mournful whistle shouts loud warnings at rural crossings, and I feel the heavy coach rock back and forth in a gentle rhythm that soothes my worn and tired spirit.

I'm alone in the dining car, save for an exuberant young porter who is singing and dancing with imaginary partners behind the stainless steel service counter. He's in a place of his own tonight, and the same is true for me. I ignore his happy performance and squint hard to see through the wide observation window into the blackness beyond. Large mercury vapor lights illuminate occasional barnyards, and the yellow glow of incandescent bulbs make the passing farmhouses seem warm and inviting against the frosty winter landscape. But the idyllic scenes appear for just a moment, then slide away as quickly as they arrive, leaving only the gleaming interior of the diner reflected in the smooth, clear window glass.

I'm not altogether familiar with the middle-aged man whose mirrored image stares back at me from the window. He reminds me of a boy I once knew, who sometimes rode the old Michigan

> **Mike VanBuren** is a Kalamazoo-based writer and bluegrass musician. In addition to camping and traveling, he enjoys creating essays and short stories, as well as occasional poems and songs. His first short story, *To Drown A Memory*, appeared in Volume II of *Voices of Michigan.*

Central rails along this same route during the late 1950's and early 1960's. But his uneven beard is streaked with gray, and his face is etched with unwelcome lines that testify to the many years and miles he has left behind. He seems eerie and out of place, like a ghostly visitor from some far-off future who has come to remind me of my own mortality. I try to look beyond him, but he mimics my movements and blocks the view. The image fades slightly whenever we pass the fleeting lights of another barnyard or farmhouse, but the stubborn apparition always returns, leaning forward with his elbows on the table and looking me straight in the eyes.

"What happened to the boy who used to ride these trains?" I ask softly, careful not to draw the scrutiny of the dancing porter. "And where's the young family that always traveled with him – the father, mother and sister?"

I used to see the boy whenever I looked into a window such as this. I remember his many hopes and dreams, and the thrill he got from watching the world flash by outside. He was the son of a railroad engineer and a trainmaster's clerk, and railroads were a big part of his young life. Many times the family traveled west from Kalamazoo to Chicago, or east to Detroit. They would skirt the backsides and underbellies of small towns and large cities, and roll through dense wood lots and across broad cornfields to destinations that seemed exotic and far away.

One Christmas season, they rode the New York Central System's *Wolverine* through Windsor, Buffalo, Syracuse, Utica, Schenectady, and Albany, then south along the Hudson River to Grand Central Station in New York City. They stayed for two days at the Piccadilly Hotel, bought hot pretzels from street vendors and attended an off-Broadway play, "Cactus Flower," that starred Betsy Palmer and Lloyd Bridges.

It was a memorable journey for the then fifteen-year-old daydreamer. He loved the thick steel platforms and heavy doors that separated the rail coaches, and enjoyed walking the long, narrow aisles to study the faces of other passengers. He was intrigued by the built-in water coolers that were located near the ends of the coaches, and he liked to drink from their conical paper cups. He particularly enjoyed watching the uniformed conductor, who came by after each stop to punch tickets and push them into narrow slots on the backs of the seats. And he pretended to travel in his own private Pullman car, imagining that the strangers he saw standing on platforms at local railroad stations had come to see him pass through their towns.

Over the years, the boy had a fair number of rail adventures. Sometimes on weekend nights, he accompanied his father to work in the Grand Rapids switchyards. He would ride in the warm locomotive, sip hot chocolate from a thermal jug and sleep on the floor of the cab when he could no longer stay awake to help with the work. Other times, he circled slowly on the revolving turntable at the aging brick roundhouse in Kalamazoo, or listened to his father swap stories with boisterous engineers, brakemen and switchmen. It was good work, being a railroad man, and one brief and glorious summer the boy tried it for himself when he hired out on the Penn Central Railroad as an eighteen-year-old locomotive fireman.

Tonight, I'm reliving those days. They were resurrected unexpectedly by the familiar odor of diesel fuel, the clicking of steel wheels on rails, and the romance of going someplace -- anyplace -- on a train. But the aging passenger in the window continues to watch me as I peer into the darkness outside, reminding me that more than thirty years have passed since the boy of my memory last rode these rails. His parents have long since retired from their railroad jobs, and the boy now has a growing family of his own. Yet the life he lived will always be a part of who I am.

The *Twilight Limited* is slowing now as it approaches Kalamazoo. I hear several more lonesome blasts from the whistle, and the conductor announces the train's imminent arrival at the picturesque depot that stands between Burdick and Rose Streets. I think about the boy arriving at this same station many years ago, jumping off the train and running ahead of his family to inspect the weathered baggage carts that lined the east end of the platform. But the narrow carts were sold to antique collectors many years ago, and the depot has been converted into a modern transportation center with a shrunken waiting room that fills with colorful vagrants on cold winter nights.

The train rolls past Western Michigan University, and the bright city lights cause the apparition to fade from the window. My thoughts broken, I stand to collect my bags and move toward the end of the coach, where the conductor is preparing the exit for passengers disembarking in what was once known as "Celery City." I lean forward to look out the window one last time as the train hisses and jerks to a stop. Outside, I see another fresh-faced boy with bright eyes and rosy cheeks who strongly resembles the one I knew so many years ago. He is standing on the snow-covered platform with his sister and mother, smiling and waving to a weary middle-aged man who is returning from Chicago.

One day, perhaps, many years from now, that boy will see his own reflection in the window of a train. And he'll remember what it was like to be a child on this night when the *Twilight Limited* brought his father home from some distant place and time.

True North

Julia Kirsten Casey

Things really fell apart for us after the miscarriage. Granted, the early part of the summer had been difficult, with me expecting, and Will's sons here for their yearly visit. But this does not compare to what happened after I lost the baby. Around the house, doing our projects and the gardening that had previously brought us so close together, we barely spoke or looked at one another.

Julia Kirsten Casey lives in Kalamazoo, Michigan. In her spare time, she enjoys gardening in the sandy soils of west Michigan, as well as her volunteer work promoting animal welfare issues. Her passion for writing began at an early age.

At the restaurant, where we both worked, it was even worse. We fought about money, employees, the menu, for God's sake. Finally, I threw up my hands and tried to keep my mouth shut about all those things. It was his place, after all, down to the last white tablecloth, water goblet, and piece of silver. It was his name on the sign over the door. *You're here to bake, Maggie,* I told myself, *just focus on the pastry.* We had been partners, perhaps not financially, but in spirit, and we weren't anymore.

Will had been so excited about the birth of our daughter, which would have been in December. All he could talk about was how wonderful it would be to bring her home in the snow, bundled up against the cold, past the Christmas lights to our little house. He was thrilled with the idea of spending the holiday with the new baby. In fact, Will had been excited since the moment I told him I was pregnant, which was not at all what I'd expected. The pregnancy hadn't been planned. We weren't married, but seconds after hearing the news, there he was, down on one knee, asking me to marry him.

I was taken with his exuberance and said, yes, even though I didn't quite feel it myself. The very idea of a baby was unsettling to me. I couldn't fathom how it would fit into our lives. The restaurant occupied much of our lives, and we had pursuits we enjoyed, no, *relied upon*, to keep us sane within the craziness of running a restaurant. We had the rituals I cherished: a glass of wine in our garden in the evenings, the leisurely Sunday morning breakfasts out, and reading our cooking magazines to each other in bed. I didn't see how a baby could fit into this reckless, brimming life that I loved. But Will, in that contagious way of his, was so ecstatic, that when he asked me to marry him, I said *yes, yes, yes*.

Those few months that I carried our baby were difficult. Not only was I wary of motherhood, but my energy was sapped, making my work as the pastry chef ten times harder. Over a short period of time, it became out of the question for me to stand ten hours a day, heft fifty-pound bags of flour, or transfer huge wads of dough from the floor mixer to the worktable. Always a hard worker, I felt diminished and frustrated.

Two months into the pregnancy, Will's twin sons arrived for their summertime visit with Dad. Queasy, exhausted, and bloated, I began to go through the motions of quasi-motherhood, none of it feeling natural, or even enjoyable. The boys regarded me with thinly veiled disdain, and demanded all of our attention, and then some. After work, it was a constant round of trips to the park, movies, and miniature golf.

My life of two months prior was nowhere to be found, and in bed late at night, I cried. I feared my life was changed forever, and I was probably right, although I never got the chance to find out.

It was a stretch for me, playing Mom, a huge stretch, and I had been counting the days until the twins would go back home to their mother out East. We were at T-minus nine days, when the bleeding started. It was early, before dawn, and I, then four months along, was in the bathroom getting ready to go to work. When I looked down and saw the blood on my thighs, running in rivulets down my legs, and finally dripping in huge splotches on the white tile floor, I let out a cry, deep and primal, but not entirely without joy. I immediately thought, my heart catching, *it's over, I'm free.*

My cry awoke Will from a dead sleep, and he says it remains burned in his memory. He heard that note of triumph in my cry and has not been able to forgive me for it. When he burst into the bathroom, I was on my knees in surprise and fear, not to mention a fair amount of pain. Will immediately came and knelt beside me. "Maggie, what's happening?" He saw all the blood then and scrambled to his feet. "Oh my God, hold on, I'll call an ambulance!" I lifted my face to him, and he stopped, seeing then the tears of joy that streaked my face. His expression changed, darkened, and has not lifted since.

I moved to the Leelanau Peninsula some weeks after the miscarriage, to a summer cottage owned by my dear friend, Peter. "Of course, darling, of course," he had said over the speakerphone from his Chicago office. "Take it for as long as you need it. I hardly get up there anymore. It will be good to have someone looking after the place." I knew deep in my heart, that my move away from Will would be a permanent one, as we now lived on separate sides of an unbridgeable chasm. What I didn't know, was where I fit in, where I belonged. Taking Peter's cottage for a little while seemed the perfect solution.

The cottage was near enough to Lake Michigan that I could feel its magnificence in the air. From the window of the sleeping loft, I could just catch a glimpse of the blue water through the trees, the lines of whitecaps endlessly moving in towards shore. The air was alive with the Lake's energy, and the west winds played over my skin during the day, and hushed me into a healing sleep at night. As I moved about the little cottage, I began to feel a little stronger. At first I did not stray far, just outside the screen door that closed with its satisfying *slap*, to walk barefoot in the sandy soil that made up the bluff the house sat upon. I could walk among the tall leafy trees to the edge and look over at the huge blue expanse of water.

One day I pulled an old bike from the shed, and giving it a once-over, deemed it worthy to ride into town. From that day on, I took daily rides over the rolling terrain of Leelanau, quickly falling in love with its treasures: the cherry orchards, the vineyards, its blue skies and bluer waters. I looked forward to my trips into town, taking a different route each time, eager to see what awaited me around each turn. It was on one of these roundabout trips to town that I found June.

There was a homemade sign tacked on the rusting farm fence that read *Kennel Help Wanted.* Interest piqued, I slowed, then stopped on my bike to more closely survey what looked like a typical farm. An old yellow farmhouse stood proud and tall in the center of it all, flanked on either side by a weathered barn. The larger of the barns was clearly used for horses, as several were grazing in its adjoining pasture. A chicken coop squatted nearby, its residents vigorously pecking the dry earth within their pen. The rolling land behind the house and outbuildings was vineyard for as far as I could see. The grapevines were tinged with gold, one of the first harbingers of fall here on Leelanau.

A smaller, graying barn stood off to the opposite side, strangely quiet and peaceful. I looked again at the help-wanted sign. *It must be old,* I thought to myself, *there don't seem to be any dogs around here.* I was about to push off again, when a woman emerged from the silent barn, six dogs trailing her. They had beautiful, sleek bodies, exquisite faces and fine bone structure, and they walked calmly and with a sense of dignity that I had never seen dogs exhibit. I was awestruck with their beauty, and I must have been staring, for the woman called out to me.

"Greyhounds," she said. "They're retired racing greyhounds. Everyone asks what they are. I'm June, by the way. I don't think I know you."

I paused for a moment, taking in this woman of indeterminate age: tanned face, strong hands, thick silver braid hanging down her back. She looked as if she had spent her lifetime working outside and enjoying every minute of it. Her face was pleasantly weathered and defined by laugh lines at the corners of her eyes and mouth. My gaze moved to the greyhounds, standing calmly in a semicircle behind her. All six of them looked at me expectantly with their soft doe eyes.

"I'm Maggie. I'm staying up the road at a friend's place," I said. "Your greyhounds are beautiful, so well behaved! I've never seen dogs like these before."

"Indeed," June said. "Greyhounds are very special animals, such gentle spirits. They suffer so much at the hands of man, at the track. You'd think their spirits would be broken. But you bring them home, and they're the most loving, trusting beings you'll ever know. It's like they know you've saved them, and they'll spend their lives being forever grateful to you." The greyhounds all stood quietly and close to June, their six heads still turned toward me, as if they were following our conversation.

"I don't understand…. you save them?"

"Oh yes," June said. "As many as I can. They put them down at the tracks by the thousands, when they lose too many races. All over the country there are organizations that rescue them, adopt them out as pets. I work with several. They bring them to me from Florida, Iowa, Wisconsin. I keep them here, fatten them up a little, and help them on their way. I help find them families."

"That's remarkable," I said, meaning it. It seemed such a selfless way for a person to spend her life. Before I knew it, I was asking about her sign: *Kennel Help Wanted*.

"The grapes will need to come in soon," June gestured toward the vineyards behind her. "And I board horses here, too. It pays the bills, you know. I'm afraid I get spread a little thin this time of year. I could use someone to help out with the greyhounds, keep up with the adoptions." She studied me hard for a moment, as if seeing me for the first time. I hadn't said anything, but it seemed she could sense my interest in working with these dogs. "Come on up to the house," she said decisively. "I have some sun tea. We can talk it over."

Late that afternoon, not having made it to town, I excitedly pedaled home with my knapsack full of books and my head bursting with information. Twenty thousand healthy greyhounds are euthanized each year in the United States because they aren't considered fast enough. As racers, greyhounds are kept in kennel crates, around the clock, with four daily turnouts for exercise and to relieve themselves. A typical dog is washed up in his career as a racer between the ages of two and five. They have never learned to play, never seen a car or the inside of a house, and never known the love of a human being.

I marveled that despite all this, they are somehow still able to trust us. I sensed the greyhounds had a lesson to teach me in resilience, and I couldn't wait to get back to June's in the morning, to start as her kennel helper.

I was to meet June outside the kennel barn at eight a.m., but in my excitement I was a few minutes early. Again, it was perfectly quiet outside the barn. She had given me a tour the previous day, and I had loved its cozy, wooden interior. It was completely weathertight, June had explained. When she first started keeping the greyhounds, an army of volunteers had helped her caulk and weatherstrip all the cracks. It is important to keep the drafts out, because greyhounds, with their short hair and lack of body fat, are susceptible to weather extremes. June had added a furnace to keep the barn warm in the cold months. Yesterday I had found it pleasantly cool, despite the heat outside.

"Mornin'," June called, striding toward me from the yellow house. She carried two cups of steaming coffee. "Didn't know how you liked your coffee, but I guessed cream and sugar." I smiled a thank you, and together we entered the barn.

June snapped on the lights and roused several greyhounds with the sudden illumination and the noise of our entering. They lifted their heads from their perches on the various old couches, armchairs, and pillows that were clustered at the center of the barn. It was like a rustic old living room with all the furniture arranged conversation-style in the central area, defined by a worn oriental area rug. A radio tuned to NPR played quietly from a corner. Several more dogs slept on, their legs splayed in the air like dead cockroaches. There were fourteen in all, and each was enjoying his or her newfound leisure. Not one moved from his or her soft spot to greet us, but we had their attention, and tails were wagging.

"Never seen a dog that liked a soft bed so much," June commented. "C'mon, lazy bones, time to go out! Then you'll get your breakfast." With that, the greyhounds were on their feet and heading toward the big barn door, moving more as a gentle flock than the stampeding pack of dogs that I expected. They passed by June and me to the fenced yard beyond, nuzzling up against us in passing. Before I knew it, all fourteen were out, playing and sniffing in the green grass. I sipped my coffee and watched them for a moment from the door. Suddenly one, a big brindled male, broke into a run along the fence line. The raw beauty and grace of a greyhound running at top speed, just for the sheer joy of it, took my breath away.

"It's quite a sight, isn't it?" June had turned to see what had caused me to gasp. Together we watched as the others joined in for a quick sprint around the yard, fourteen lithe bodies in motion. "Somehow I never get tired of it."

I did not tire of it, either. I spent the remaining sultry days of summer learning the ropes around the kennel. There were the twice-daily feedings, and each dog got a little one-on-one playtime and attention. I had an "office" in a converted stall in the kennel barn where I managed the web site: posting dogs' pictures and information, retrieving completed online adoption forms, and answering e-mails. The phone rang surprisingly often with inquiries about adoption. Together, June and I interviewed potential adopters, either by phone or in person. It was up to me to check the references and make follow-up calls to people who had already adopted. From their spots on the couches, the greyhounds lazily watched me do all this.

By Labor Day, I was an old hand at walking four greys at a time into town to give them exposure to the public. June had already succeeded at cultivating an awareness of the greyhounds' plight among the townsfolk; many had already adopted one. Some had even acquired two or three, over time. It was my job to increase awareness among the tourists that often visited town, and all I had to do was appear with my four beautiful greyhounds, two leashes in each hand. As I stood in the shaded park in town, people approached, full of questions about the greys. I carried brochures printed with greyhound information, cards listing our phone number and web site, and I answered as many questions as I could.

"They need to be kept on a leash at all times," I explained time and time again. "Their instinct is to chase, and if they see a squirrel, a rabbit, or even a paper cup blowing down the road, they might chase it. And since they run at 45 miles per hour, you wouldn't have a chance of catching them."

"Greyhounds make excellent house pets," I extolled, "They're good with children, eager to please. A fenced yard is nice, but isn't required. A couple of walks a day will do for exercise."

The work with the greyhounds was all-consuming, and only rarely did I think about Will or the restaurant, and even then, those were fleeting thoughts. Undoubtedly, I felt complete on Leelanau, in the presence of these magnificent beings. For the first time since the miscarriage, the uneasiness of my desire to remain childless lifted. Watching June and her way in the world had reassured me that all was right within. I felt at once clean and clear in my purpose, focused like a laser. Eight of the original fourteen greyhounds had been adopted, and my heart had never been lighter.

I think June could see my transformation, too. Lately, out of the corner of my eye, I saw her looking at me, smiling and shaking her head. "When are you going to pick yours?" she asked one day.

"They're all mine," I answered, dodging her question. I'd actually been giving it a lot of thought, but I'd concluded that I'd know when the time was right. The cottage was Peter's, and I didn't feel right about moving a dog in without asking him. June smiled knowingly. The woman could practically read my mind.

A week later, ten more greyhounds arrived at the farm, fresh off a track in Florida. This was my first experience with newly retired racers, but June, who'd been through this countless times, helped me all the way. Since there were so many, we decided to clip temporary tags to their collars, identifying them by their racing names. Later we'd come up with more sensible names for them, as racing names are usually long and impractical to use. I watched as June began to write the names with Magic Marker on the paper tags-- *Bailey's Comet, Rated G, Smoke Signal.* Then I turned to watch the six resident greyhounds making friends with the newcomers.

"Are greys always this good-natured with each other?" I interrupted June's writing. I had been concerned that the arrival of ten new greyhounds would upset the peace in the barn, at least for a little while, but clearly the dogs accepted each other. Some of the newcomers had already found a comfy spot.

She looked up from the tags. "Generally, yes. You should see them at the greyhound reunion we have each year. They act like they're long lost friends, even though most of them haven't met. They have a special kinship. You can tell."

The rest of the day was packed with activity. Together, June and I bathed each of the ten newcomers and administered flea medication. The town veterinarian stopped by after lunch to check them out, more out of interest than necessity, as the greyhounds had received their vaccinations and spay or neuter surgeries before leaving Florida. I walked my legs off, leading each one outside every hour as part of the housebreaking routine. Most of them already seemed to realize the proper place to go, but we kept them on close watch, just to make sure. At the end of the day, June dragged out more big pillows and blankets to ensure there wouldn't be any competition for soft beds.

"Tomorrow," June declared as I was leaving, exhausted, at nine p.m., "we'll take some of them into the house and teach them to walk up and down the stairs." I knew from the books she'd loaned me that greyhounds, having lived in the racing kennel all their lives, had no idea about stairs. I nodded, thinking this sounded like even harder work than we'd done today. My muscles felt pleasantly sore as I climbed aboard my bike and pedaled toward the cottage.

That night I awoke to the sound of thunder in the distance and the waves of Lake Michigan lashing the shore. As I pulled aside the limp cotton curtain next to my bed, lightning flashed somewhere out over the Lake, still far away. I threw back the covers the rest of the way, hauled myself out of bed, and quickly dressed in the clothes I'd abandoned on the floor only a few hours before. For good measure, I grabbed a clean sweatshirt from the pile and put that on, too. I thought the new greyhounds might be uneasy in their new surroundings, with the storm coming and all, and I wanted to be with them.

As I drove my car the short distance to the farm, rain began to fall, so I switched on the windshield wipers and the high beams. The wind was angrily whipping the trees, and thunder rumbled again, louder, and closer this time.

Damp from the rain, I burst through the kennel barn door, and clicked on the overhead light. The dogs were clustered on the furniture and the pillows on the floor, some taking the storm in stride, others nervously huddled together. All were awake, though, and their eyes followed me in the darkness, after I shut off the light and made my way to the pillow-covered floor space in the center of the couches and chairs. I pulled a blanket off the back of a couch and comfortably settled myself among the cushions. "Hi, guys," I said. "Everything's all right." Three fearful dogs came to my side. One by one, I felt them settle in beside me, tucking themselves in close. One rested his head heavily on my thigh, and pretty soon I felt a small greyhound body curl itself in the crook of my arm. I stroked her shaking body with my other hand, until, after a while she quieted, then dared to unbury her head from my armpit. As the storm passed, she placed her graceful head on my chest, over my heart.

I awoke to June's voice and bright golden sunlight streaming in through the barn door. Greyhounds were still tucked around me in their sleeping postures, the little female included, her head still resting on my chest. In the light of day, I could see she had beautiful fawn coloring. I lifted my head and smiled at June, a little sheepish to be found sleeping among the greyhounds. The little fawn female lifted her head, too.

"Are you going to sleep all day?" June called cheerily. She had a newspaper section folded in a square and a steaming cup of coffee in her hand. "Breakfast's ready. We'll let the dogs out while we eat. Then after we get everyone fed, we've got to get a move on!" She waved the newspaper square in the air.

"Get going? I thought we were going to start teaching them stair climbing." I yawned and scratched the fawn greyhound under the chin; her eyelids lowered in pleasure.

"That can wait a day. They only have these open houses on Sundays," she responded. I could now see that she had circled some of the real estate listings. As I let my hand drift to the little grey's collar, I smiled at the way June knew me to my depths. My fingers found her paper tag, and I twisted it on its string so I could read her name: *True North*. "Are you coming or not, lazy bones?"

In that split second I'd made my decision. Yes, yes, *yes*, I was coming. No hesitation or trepidation this time, just True North by my side as I scrambled to my feet to join June in the Leelanau sunshine.

Voices of Michigan

The Eagle

Dave Stegehuis

For some time I wondered why I journeyed to the lakes, fields, and forests to pursue fish and wild game. It all started early. At age ten, I often trekked to an undeveloped area near our home which included a small pond, a large shallow lake, rolling hills covered with scrub oak, and abandoned farmland grown over with weeds and brush. In all, there were about five square miles of roadless wildlife habitat. Sometimes alone, at other times with a friend, I set traps around the lake for muskrats in the winter and in the fields for fox in the fall. The trapline had to be tended twice a day and presented an opportunity for me to spend many hours in the outdoors interacting with wild creatures in the natural places where they lived.

Dave Stegehuis, a lifelong resident of Michigan, retired from teaching after thirty-five years in the classroom. Since last March, he has been writing a bi-monthly column called "Outdoors" for the local newspaper, *The Lowell Ledger.* The column allows Dave to create interest in the outdoors.

My late father grew up in northern Michigan at a time when fishing and hunting were a necessary part of daily living. The streams and forests provided the family with a food source to supplement farm-raised crops and animals. I would listen with great interest as he recounted his adventures in the woods around Cross Village, near the tip of the Lower Peninsula, early in the last century. One story was about how, as a small boy, he would carry a large burlap sack to put fish in when his brothers speared redhorse suckers during the spring spawning run. He told another tale about trading a bicycle for an old 410 shotgun, and using it to hunt the brown and white dappled jackrabbits that inhabited a deep and forbidding cedar swamp. When we were old enough, my brother and I accompanied our father on new outdoor adventures around our home in southwestern Michigan and on very special trips when we traveled "Up North," as we called any place north of White Cloud. It was during these excursions that I became committed to an outdoor lifestyle.

I began hunting when I was twelve years old, first hunting rabbits and pheasants, and then a few years later, I graduated to stalking the elusive whitetail deer with bow and arrow. I haven't trapped animals since I was a young boy, but have continued to hunt and fish without interruption ever since. When fall arrives, I get restless, and a strange longing draws me to the fields and woods.

Nevertheless—wildlife management issues aside—why would I find it necessary to hunt and kill the beautiful and graceful whitetail deer, the brilliantly plumed ring-necked pheasant, or the swift and resourceful ruffed grouse? Why spend glorious fall days scouting new areas for game sign, building blinds, and planning hunting strategy? The wild game does provide food for family and friends, but then twenty minutes down the road there is a supermarket well-stocked with poultry, pork, and beef. Someone else has gone to the trouble of raising, butchering, and packaging these and other domesticated animals. It's just a matter of taking a few minutes to make a selection, flash a plastic card, and you're on your way. Why bother to get out of a warm bed on a cold morning well before the sun begins to peek over the eastern horizon? Why wander through the damp dark woods, only to climb into a tree and sit in its branches to wait for daylight and the possibility of a deer coming into bow range? Why devote valuable time to practicing with bow or gun when there are so many other forms of recreation and entertainment today?

I do know that I love animals and the places where they live. But, I can go out and sit in the woods and enjoy nature by observation or through photography. There are many nature trails and parks for the public to enjoy. These areas provide opportunities to get plenty of fresh air and exercise which many of us find so elusive in these busy times. I can hike scenic trails, camp in a variety of natural settings, and swim in the lakes. The fact is, it's still possible to get close to nature without taking animals. So why hunt? This was a question that I began asking myself more often as I grew older.

On a particularly cool and clear morning last fall, I quietly made my way through the woods well before daylight, as I had done on countless other mornings. My entire world was confined to the narrow beam of a small flashlight. The footing was precarious as I negotiated the steep hillside terminating at the bank of a picture-postcard river that wound through the southwestern Michigan farm country.

My destination was a ground blind from which I would patiently wait with my bow and arrow for the arrival of a whitetail deer. The blind was made of dead tree limbs, and store-bought camouflage material, and was equipped with a folding campstool for comfort. The plan was to ambush a whitetail buck as he returned to heavy cover where he would spend the daylight hours after feeding all night in the nearby fields. After settling into the blind, it was almost an hour before I noticed the first rays of sunlight begin to slowly reveal the dark shapes of the trees and the contour of the ground around me. As if on cue, the woods began to awaken with the occasional hammering of a pileated woodpecker, the gobble of a distant wild turkey, and the rustle of leaves under small feet as red squirrels searched the forest floor for breakfast. As more of the local residents joined in, the activity increased to a point where the commotion was enough to drown out the sound of the river as it flowed around ancient rocks and storm-toppled trees. The symphony caused me to become more relaxed and somewhat drowsy, making it difficult to stay focused on the task of listening and watching for the expected buck deer.

A rush of adrenaline jolted my senses to full alert when a subtle movement drew my attention to a whitetail doe approaching on the deer-trail near my blind. The deer moseyed by, unaware that I was there. Later a pair of mink exited the river right in front of me and scampered up a small feeder creek to the safety of a den hidden in the bank.

Just about then, a movement out over the river diverted my attention. I looked up in time to see a large bird make a 180 degree turn, fly downstream and drop to skim the surface of the river in front of my blind. With a few strong wing beats, it swiftly lifted off and flew up into a tall oak located only a few yards from my hiding place. I immediately froze my movement and shifted my eyes—which were hidden by a veil of camouflage netting—to see a bald eagle with something in its talons sitting on a short dead branch above me. I couldn't believe my good fortune, getting so close to a wild bald eagle. Eagles were almost non-existent in this area for many years, and I had never been this close to one. I had only observed the great birds at a distance soaring on the wind, or sometimes gliding down to snatch prey off the surface of a lake.

The blind and my camouflage clothing apparently masked my presence from the large predator on the limb. Enthralled, I watched as it rearranged its grip on what appeared to be a small bass that it had just plucked from the river. I continued to watch as it dined on its early morning prize. The bird tore pieces off the fish with its large yellow beak until there was nothing left. I was amazed that it didn't drop a morsel.

Even though the eagle still didn't know I was there, I figured the bird would soon fly away and go about its business. After a while, it was apparent that it wasn't going to leave right away. Then it occurred to me that the eagle was waiting for a fish or other prey to expose itself to its intense surveillance. As I looked over the eagle's shoulder, I could see its head slowly turn from side to side as it continued to monitor the area.

All at once the significance of this tableau washed over me like a wave: we were both hunting! I felt a kinship, a closeness to this wild creature that I had never before experienced in over a half-century of outdoor observation. After comprehending the situation, I purposefully shifted my attention back to the task at hand and refocused my senses to seek my own quarry: a whitetail buck. I felt honored to share this wild place with this majestic creature, and by continuing to pursue my own prey I could prolong the experience. There seemed to be a sense of common purpose between us. Although, as a hunter, I don't presume to be worthy of being counted in the same league with this strong and skillful predator. I was determined to continue hunting as long as the eagle remained at its post.

About mid-morning, the great bird pushed off from the limb, spread its wings, and slowly gained altitude as it flew upstream to continue its quest for survival. That morning I was able to, without any doubt, finally answer the question: Why do I hunt? Hunting with the eagle made me acutely aware of my relationship with the earth and its creatures. For a short period of time I had the feeling of being an integral part of nature and not just an observer, not an intruder, but a legitimate participant in the circle of life. The deer, the fish, the eagle, and I were all equal, one not being more important than the other, but each with our own predetermined roll to play in a drama written long ago.

There is one big difference, however, between the eagle and me: the eagle continued to hunt that morning, while I, on the other hand, didn't see the buck; so when I got tired of sitting in that blind, I gave up and went home. You see, I could stop hunting because I have a pension, and the supermarket is just down the street.

Stallion Wannabes

Emily Meier

I am a generic girl. Or as Tom Petty would say, An American Girl, one who loves horses. I am no different from the millions of girls who, at ten years of age, wanted a horse more than their next breath. Day and night I dreamed of owning my own horse. I prayed to God for a horse and wished on stars for a horse in case God was too busy.

> **Emily Meier** is the product of a Michigan summer love affair. She has been writing for as long as she can remember. More recently she has been published in *The Smart Girl's Guide to College*. Emily has also done free-lance work for *The Grosse Pointe News*.

I read books about girls who owned horses. In elementary school, I ordered every horse book and poster that Weekly Reader had. I recited verbatim from my horse books on how to care for a horse to anyone who would listen. I played "horse" with a mop-handled horse head, pretending, hoping it would come to life. Sometimes I covered it in Band-Aids, or pretended to pick its hooves, testing out what it might be like to be a veterinarian--for horses, of course.

Other times I slipped out of my rubber uglies (good shoes for mucking out stalls) and clopped around in clogs behind the house, convincing the neighborhood kids that I had a horse in the garage. On one particular day it worked so well that I had at least ten neighborhood kids convinced I was a horse owner. Soon, so were their parents. Our house was flooded with calls from "concerned neighbors" who weren't convinced a garage in the suburbs was the best place to keep such a large animal. This particular incident, mixed with hope that my horse obsession could be cured or at least diluted, convinced my parents it was time: I was old enough for a sleep-away horse camp.

It was heaven. Sleep-away horse camp was a twenty-four-hour-a-day horse-a-thon. I helped feed them before dawn. I rode them all morning and most of the afternoon. Then, on my free period, I would climb up on a pasture fence rail and watch them. I learned their colors and markings, picking them out by their stars, stripes, and blazes. I learned which ones were friends and which ones weren't. I learned about the "pecking order" and watched the scuffles as they nipped, kicked, and chased each other, constantly redefining their status in the herd. I learned the Clydesdale, despite his great size, was not necessarily king of the pasture. Indeed, that summer, a small but very feisty Shetland pony named Peanut was king. Peanut ruled alone while the others fought for the positions directly under him. Second in command was an ever-changing position, sometimes held by an Appaloosa named Apollo or a crotchety bay named Buckshot. Each position after that had an even larger number of contenders vying for the spot. I loved to watch them buck and gallop. Free of saddles and other human constraints, they would shake their heads and kick up their back legs, the wind blowing through their manes and tails. So big and yet so elegant, they pranced and played, chests puffed out and heads held high. A pasture full of stallion wannabes.

Sleep-away horse camp came to an end all too quickly. I said good-bye to my new friends, and all the horses, and reluctantly joined my family at our summer home on Crooked Lake. There, among extended family, I found myself once again in the minority, as one of the only girls in the male-dominated summer world of relatives. I tried to keep up with my cousins, the boys, but they didn't want to hear about all-girl sleep-away horse camp. They didn't care what I had learned about horses. I was constantly being left behind or told to go home. So, I ended up watching them from a distance.

I watched as they raced each other to see who could swim across the lake and back. I watched as they competed in the tin boats to see who had the fastest motor. I watched as they spit watermelon seeds to see who could spit the farthest. I watched from inside the boat as my cousin Jeff, just twelve years old, hung on to a ski rope for thirty minutes and became the first and only kid ever to ski from Pickerel Lake to Crooked Lake. I watched as they raced sailboats, skied buoys, pegged swans with rocks, fished for the biggest fish, burped and farted louder, wore a bathing suit the longest, went for the most days without a bath, fought, wrestled, and kicked. Like watching the horses from the pasture fence, I learned which of my cousins were really friends and which ones were just vying for a higher position in the herd.

Once when I was little, I practiced moving my eyes like a horse in a mirror. I imitated how my aunt's horse had looked after being stung by a bee, eyes wide, nostrils flared.

I thought I had it down, but when I went to show my dad, he just laughed, "You're not a horse," he said.

"I know," I said, rolling my eyes more like the little girl I was. I wasn't trying to *be* a horse.

I triumphed at fifteen. I had saved every penny I ever acquired—babysitting, lemonade stands, birthdays, Christmas, allowance--since I was seven. I saved it all, not for a rainy day, but for a horse. My parents were impressed and a bit overwhelmed that my horse obsession was still as strong, despite years of sleep-away horse camp. We had the you-can-break-your-neck-and-become-a-paraplegic discussion a final time, and then my parents broke down. "Ok," they said, "we'll help you find a horse."

It took months of searching, but on a cloudy day in early spring I found Jimmy. He was a beautiful reddish-brown gelding, seven years old, and trained to be ridden in both English and Western fashion. He had a little jumping experience and a bit of preliminary dressage training. We hit it off immediately, and within hours I had my own horse. The only dream I ever had came true.

I got even more horse books. I was petrified that I wouldn't know how to care for him properly, that I would make some mistake and jeopardize his health. I researched barns and trainers.

I took lessons and listened to the barn ladies, who seemed to know everything about all things horsey.

Sometimes I sat in the grass outside the pasture where Jimmy roamed and grazed with twenty other horses, all geldings. I watched to see where he fit in the pecking order. He usually secured himself a top spot, which made me feel proud. He had spirit. One day while I was sitting on the grass watching him chase off another horse, my friend called to me because our lesson was starting.

I got Jimmy's halter and a lead rope and made my way to the gate of the pasture where he was. Hoping for food, or perhaps a bit of human attention, the horses began to gather. I soon found myself staring into at least a dozen pairs of eyes as the group of horses started to cram together at the fence. I had to push on the gate and shoo them back. I called to Jimmy, who pushed his way through the crowd of hairy rumps and swishing tails. Here's the thing about the pecking order: The more confined the herd, the more intense it becomes. I knew this and was hurrying to buckle Jimmy's halter into place and get away from the increasing crowd of horses, but it was already too late. One horse in the back bit another on the rump, which then made that horse kick out, hitting another, and within seconds, the rippling effect of the pecking order reached me and Jimmy, slamming him against me, and me against the electric fence, which in turn shocked us both. Being zapped by an electric fence is a nuisance for a twelve-hundred pound horse, but for a hundred-pound girl, it is a hair-raising experience. Despite feeling dizzy, and wondering if the faint smell of something burning was my insides, I managed to get Jimmy out of the pasture and saddled for my lesson. The others in the barn laughed and patted me on the back as I told them what had happened. They too had experienced the Pecking Order, first hand.

The summer after finding Jimmy, I was even more reluctant to make the annual journey with my family to Crooked Lake for extended family fun. I didn't want to leave him behind. I had dreams of trailing Jimmy along and riding him into the lake after a long gallop. However, keeping Jimmy at our cottage would be like keeping a horse in the garage of a suburban home, fun to imagine but completely unrealistic. I made arrangements with the barn, making sure he would be cared for while I was away. Once again, I found myself pulled away from the horse world and thrust back into a world of boys.

I read books on them, too. I tried to learn to sail, improve my water skiing ability, and muster up some sort of excitement for spitting and pegging swans with rocks, but despite my best efforts, I was still told to go home or ignored altogether. It hurt, maybe not as much as the electric fence, but it stung.

As a sophomore in college, I was forced to sell Jimmy. I was away too much, and he needed more care than I was able to give him while trying to balance studies and a social life. Selling him was one of the hardest things I have ever done. That summer, horseless and too old to return to sleep-away horse camp, I spent more time on Crooked Lake with the boys. Surprisingly, it wasn't too bad. We were older, and we seemed to get along better. Sometimes they even asked me to go along for a sail or a ski.

However, at the height of the season, when the houses on Crooked Lake reached full capacity, things got tense. I had a flashback to the day in the pasture with Jimmy, the crowd moving in, the ears flattening, the nip that starts it all. Not one to get zapped twice, I retreated, giving the boys time to peck out their own order. I had learned my lesson. I watched from a distance as they puffed out their chests and lifted their heads. They got into a few scuffles, and one of my aunts explained it away with a shrug. "Boys will be boys," she said. And horses will be horses, I thought, and I am just a girl who loves them.

Voices of Michigan

One of God's Fishermen

Mary L. Rupe

When the phone rang, I dried my hands on a dishtowel and picked up the receiver. It was late morning, and I couldn't imagine who was calling. I instantly wondered if it was about my son, Tommy.

"Mrs. Kercher?" queried a male voice.

"Yes, I'm Mrs. Kercher," I answered.

"Your neighbors, the Poscharscky's, asked me to call you. They had an accident last night," the man said.

"What? Where? How bad? Was anybody hurt?" I asked, dreading to hear the reply.

As I listened, the calming male voice explained, "The family's camper was overturned by strong winds on Interstate 65,

> **Mary L. Rupe** is a graduate of the Institute of Children's Literature and is currently a student of the Long Ridge Writers Group. As a child she dreamed of writing the "Great American Novel"…a page turner…destined to become required reading for all American literature courses.

just south of Columbus. There were no serious injuries, only bruises and lacerations; except for David. He died of a cerebral hemorrhage."

I gasped, "Oh my! Is there anything I can do?"

"No, everything's being taken care of," answered the man. "Friends are driving the family home tomorrow, and Yoder-Culp Funeral Home is making the arrangements for David's body. Mr. Poscharscky wanted you to know before the story made today's newspaper. He hoped you'd find the right words to tell Tommy."

"Thank you for calling. Please give them our love, and assure them that I'll break the news to Tommy. Also thank them for thinking of Tommy at this time. Please, if there's anything more I can do, have someone call me." I hung up the receiver and finished the breakfast dishes on autopilot. The words of David's death echoed in my mind. Without conscious thought I prayed, "Lord, help me find the strength and the right words to tell my son."

Tommy and David were eight-year-old best friends from different families. They were closer than Siamese twins. David was a blue-eyed, tow-headed lad, and Tommy had green eyes, freckles, and a mop of red hair. Visions of Little League, Cub Scouts, backyard campouts, school, and fishing kaleidoscopically whirled in my head. What words would help my son understand that he'd never fish with his best friend again? How could I explain to Tommy what I didn't understand myself?

"Mom?" Tommy called as the screen door announced his arrival.

"I'm in the kitchen. Come help me with the lemonade and cookies; we'll have a picnic down by the willows."

"Okey dokey, but first I gotta mark another day off the calendar. David'll be home tomorrow. I can hardly wait! Gosh, he's been gone a zillion days," said Tommy as he marked an X through the seventeenth of July. "Mom, are you okay? You look kinda funny."

"I'm okay," I said, wondering what the penalty is for lying at a time like this. "Please carry this tray of cookies out by the willows. I'll bring the lemonade."

The walk to the willow-shaded picnic table seemed endless. I felt like I was pushing a piece of cooked spaghetti up hill. My tears and pain threatened to unleash their fury. Again, I prayed for the strength and the right words, as my shaking hands set down the rattling tray. As Tommy crumbled snicker doodles for the mallards, I wondered just how to begin. My eyes scanned the backyard landscape and settled on *The Fish Fryer*, Tommy and David's rowboat. That's when the words came to me.

"Tommy, you know what a good fisherman David is, right?"

"Yeah, so…"

"Well, God knows that, too. And knowing what luck and skill David has, God has chosen him to be one of his special fishermen," I explained. "David won't be going fishing with you anymore, he's gone to heaven…."

"But, Mom," Tommy started.   Then, as my words took root, he shouted, "God can't do that! David and I are best friends! We're blood brothers, just like the Lone Ranger and Tonto. When we grow up, we're gonna run the orchard for Grandpa. Why did God do this?"

"Now Tommy, I'm sure David didn't want to leave you behind. I know you'll miss him, but as long as he's in here," I said tapping on his chest, "you'll always have him with you. It won't be the same, but…."

"Mom, it's not right! David is only eight years old! Why does God have to be so mean?" Tears flooded my son's green eyes.

"God isn't mean, Tommy. We may not always like what he does, but think about your Bible stories, doesn't God know best?"

Tommy sat in silence, his tears speaking mute volumes. "You're right, Mom," he sighed as last. "Tell me what happened."

"David's family had an accident. Their camper turned over, and David died of a cerebral hemorrhage (that's broken blood vessels in the brain). His sisters and parents escaped with only minor cuts and bruises. They'll be home tomorrow. Friends are driving them from Columbus in southern Indiana where the accident happened. The funeral will be on Saturday."

"Did David hurt a lot?" Tommy asked.

"No, God took his pain away," I answered.

Tommy gave it some thought, then asked, "Mom, will the funeral be like Grandma's? Remember, I talked to her and told her goodbye."

"Yes, Tommy, I remember. When we go to the funeral, you can talk to David and tell him goodbye or whatever you want. I know David's mom and dad won't mind."

Gathering the remnants of our forgotten picnic, I felt my son's arms encircle my waist. "I love you, Mom," he said, squeezing tightly.

"I love you, Tommy," I whispered, as I returned his bear hug.

We wiped our eyes, as we both tried to comprehend the fact that David wouldn't be coming home.

"Mom, I'd like to sit in *The Fish Fryer*, if that's okay?" asked Tommy.

"Sure, honey, just don't leave the dock." I returned, carrying the picnic remains to the kitchen, and watched Tommy from the window. Although no sound reached my ears, I could see his lips moving. There was little doubt that David and God were in for a serious interrogation from my son.

Tommy sat dockside in the rowboat until dusk. I knew he had to deal with the loss of his best friend in his own way. I just wasn't sure what his way would be.

As I tucked my freckled-faced son in for the night, he asked, "Mom, can the fishing picture of me and David be moved to my night stand?" Not bothering to answer, I quickly granted his request, setting the picture in the place of honor. I looked from the two smiling lads holding aloft their prized catch, to the pair of teary green eyes that looked up at me, and my own tears started once again.

Tommy whispered, "It's okay, Mom. David, God, and me had a long talk today, and I know that David's gonna be the best of God's fishermen."

"I love you, Tommy," was all my tightened throat allowed me to say.

The Gift of Love

Richard Blackmer

The small scrap of paper slipped from her hand and drifted silently to the floor. Slowly Wanda lowered herself until she was seated on the edge of the bed. Her heart, filled with a mother's love, which the passage of years could not diminish, desperately wanted to believe. Her mind did not.

> **Richard Blackmer** is an editor and writer for a community newspaper. In addition to his own journalistic responsibilities, he has been published in the *Ensign* magazine, the *Canadian Messenger* of the Sacred Heart and *West Michigan Today*. Richard and Rachel, married for thirty-three years, reside in Grand Haven, Michigan.

Her mind argued that Chiquita had been gone for many years. And the argument was true. It had been over a decade since the death of her only daughter.

Logic reminded Wanda that on two occasions, since the loss of Chiquita, Wanda had changed her place of residence. Both changes contributed to the winnowing of Chiquita's possessions. Now, only those few possessions remained which were the most intimate reminders of her daughter's life.

Every one of the remaining items which had been Chiquita's during her brief twenty-five years on earth, was now a repository for a cherished memory of a mother's first born. As a mother, Wanda had lovingly guarded each. She was always careful to replace those precious reminders in a secure place after revisiting the memories they guarded. Never at any time were any of them left haphazardly lying around. Never at any time, prior to this day, had she even seen this small piece of paper.

As in times past, when the pain of her loss became unbearable, Wanda's heart became her shield and her encouragement, and so it was now. Her heart, which cradled a mother's undying love for a child, urged her to look upon the paper again. She slowly lowered her eyes to the floor and focused on the paper.

The small piece of paper bore only two thoughts: a single word--Christmas--and a single date--1977. It was not the message that caused her heart to leap within. It was the handwriting. The handwriting was Chiquita's. Even Wanda's mind, which denied the actuality of this piece of paper suddenly appearing from nowhere, offered no challenge to its authorship.

The countless hours of searching through Chiquita's books and clothing and personal effects had never revealed the existence of this piece of paper. Yet today, when the burden of grief seemed to be at its greatest, a message of comfort came in the form of a piece of paper, a piece of paper found mysteriously lying on a table in an unused guest room.

Her mind again decried the sanity of believing such a possibility. However, her heart, dismissing any further denial, embraced the joy of acceptance, and Wanda reached to the floor to retrieve the paper. She held it tightly in her hand and pressed it close to her bosom. The comforting presence of the message radiated a bittersweet ecstasy to her soul.

This was the second experience. The second time, when her desperation and pain were so great, that comfort came from a seemingly miraculous source.

Still clutching the scrap of paper, with moistened eyes, she traced her thoughts back to the first experience. It was during her visit to Carmel after Chiquita's death.

Chiquita had loved California, particularly Carmel with its famous cliff-side tree. A friend, knowing of Chiquita's sentiment, had sketched the tree and made a gift of the drawing to Chiquita. In Chiquita's darkest hours, as she fought the pain and the ravaging effects of disease, Chiquita had derived comfort from the drawing.

To share a visit to the tree with her mother had been one of Chiquita's fondest desires. However, it was not until after Chiquita's death that Wanda was able to make the trip to Carmel.

Perhaps it was divine providence that caused the delay. For the visit to the tree had opened her heart to the omnipotent power of love: the power of love to pierce the veil of death and send comfort to one who has endured terrible loss.

Wanda recalled that day in Carmel, the day of the first experience. Wanda had sat transfixed on the bus, every ounce of her consciousness focused on the tree, her mind attempting to memorize its every feature, and her soul seeking to capture every feeling that Chiquita had experienced. It was as if her spirit reached back through time on this very spot where Chiquita had been and bonded anew with her daughter. The intensity of the moment permitted only a vague awareness of the tour guide's dissertation to the other tourists.

Suddenly there was silence. Slowly, Wanda refocused on the interior of the bus. Awareness came to her that the narration had stopped. She moved her gaze from the tree to the front of the bus, and allowed it to rest on the tour guide.

The guide silently stood with microphone in hand. The eyes of the guide, no longer on the tree, rested fully on Wanda.

A gentle smile crossed the face of the tour guide, and with an empathic softening of her features, she raised the microphone to her lips.

Respectfully, almost reverently, the tour guide spoke: "The tree must have a great deal of meaning to this lady, for her eyes have not left it since we arrived."

Wanda sat receptively as every head turned in her direction; through respectful silence, the entire bus paid homage to her moment of spiritual reunion.

Now Wanda allowed her thoughts to return to the present, to the edge of the bed, to her joys for the day. She would soon be taking her granddaughter to the mall, but first, Wanda lowered her clenched hand from her bosom, and slowly opened her fingers. Her eyes, clouded with tears, could no longer focus on the paper. She gently closed her eyes to the world and allowed her spirit to explore the omnipresence of love.

Once again, she pressed the small piece of paper to her breast. Her mind created a collage of memories, a patchwork of remembrances alternately celebrating the life of her beloved daughter, and then, once again, subjecting her to the excruciating pain of loss.

Rising slowly to her feet, Wanda relived, as countless times before, the blessed moments of closeness that she had shared with Chiquita.

Throughout the day, as Wanda readied herself to take her granddaughter to the mall, her thoughts stayed on the experience. She asked the same questions a hundred times over. Where did the piece of paper come from? How did it get into the guestroom?

Amid ambling shoppers, Wanda stood, holding her granddaughter's hand. They both admired the mall Christmas tree. Christmas had always been a favorite of Chiquita's. Wanda wondered if Chiquita was aware that it was Christmas time here in mortality? She wondered if Chiquita was aware of her great pain? Was she aware of the unfillable void her death had created?

"Grandma, I want that one!" Her granddaughter's exclamation interrupted Wanda's thoughts, and returned her mind to the task at hand. Her granddaughter had identified an ornament on the great Christmas tree. The ornament was remote, out of the way, a nondescript ornament, an ornament which, by comparison, should have gone unnoticed. Yet her granddaughter, motivated by some inexplicable reason, had selected this very one from the thousand others on the tree.

Wanda requested that the attendant remove the ornament from the tree. On the underside of the ornament a name would be inscribed, the name of a child who would not have a Christmas this year. Wanda and her granddaughter would purchase a gift for the named child and place it under the tree for delivery on Christmas Eve. It was a simple, benevolent gesture to help one child experience a better Christmas.

Wanda accepted the retrieved ornament from the attendant, and with her granddaughter's eager expectation, she turned the ornament bottom side up to read the name.

Her heart leaped within her. Her hand trembled, and her voice broke, as she read the name inscribed on the bottom of the ornament: Chiquita.

Wanda stood silently as tears streamed down her face. "Yes," she spoke softly to herself, "Chiquita is aware." Aware that it is Christmas time, aware of her mother's loneliness, aware of her mother's pain.

A smile slowly etched the corners of Wanda's mouth, displaying for all the world to see, her understanding of this special gift, this acknowledging gift of her daughter's eternal love, a love equal to her own, a love so strong that it even transcends the separation of death.

Wanda's troubled heart found peace.

(A graduate of Radford College, Chiquita Lynn Candler devoted her short life to helping troubled youth as a probation officer in the Virginia juvenile court system. Chiquita passed away, at the age of twenty-five, on February 20, 1980 after a ten year struggle with Hodgkin's disease.)

The Helm

Matthew C. Brown

It was a day like this when my grandfather and I took our last sail together: a radiant afternoon with golden sunbeams refracting off the festoons of cresting waves. Cottony clouds merged and parted in the sky. Lake Michigan dimpled with moving shadows.

> **Matthew C. Brown**, a native of Michigan, lives in Chicago, where he is an assistant editor for *The Rotarian* Magazine. He is currently working on a collection of short stories about Ecuador.

My grandfather wouldn't die for another year, but already I sensed the cancer running through his body, gnawing at his bone. He was weak—tired too; and yet his eyes were still wide with anticipation as we motored through the channel. "I think we are going to have a fine sail," he said. "A real fine sail."

We both looked at Big Red, Holland Harbor's famous lighthouse. It appeared freshly painted against the backdrop of pale blue sky. A long pole sprung from the lighthouse turret. At the top, a huge American flag undulated in the freshening northwest wind. My grandfather squinted as he studied the flag. "Twelve to fifteen," he said in reference to the wind speed. "Maybe a few gusts to eighteen."

I smiled. All my life, when I sailed with my grandfather, he'd report the wind conditions. That American flag had always been his indicator, though I'd never quite figured out how he knew the difference between twelve and fifteen, or fifteen and eighteen.

We cleared the mouth of the channel and were now in the cobalt water of Lake Michigan. I raised the main, unfurled the jib. Then my grandfather turned off the engine; this has always been my favorite nautical moment: the grind of the diesel replaced by the tinkle of halyards on the mast, the stretch of sheets, and the soothing gurgle of water around the hull.

My grandfather loved that moment, too. He thrummed his fingers on the fiberglass, regarding the sails carefully. "Looks pretty good. Maybe we could ease the traveler a bit, though." He always found rigging to tweak, adjustments to make.

The traveler eased, I settled opposite my grandfather in the cockpit. The wind had ruffled his curls; they twisted atop his head like whitecaps. He moistened his lips with his tongue while he held the tiller in his big, meaty hands. I knew this was how I would always remember him: seated at the helm, his gentle eyes— with brows raised as if he were listening to an old friend speak— scanning the horizon.

The first time I ever sailed was with my grandfather, on his thirty-foot Pearson, *Charlest II*. I was only about seven months old, so, of course, I don't remember it. During the ensuing twenty-three summers, we plied these waters, reaching and tacking, skirting Michigan's western shore. He showed me how to tie a bowline, to read telltales, and how to set an anchor. I marveled at the way he moved about the cockpit; he was smooth, almost athletic, as he ground winches and tamed the flapping sails.

We'd stay out on the lake for hours at a time. When we were hungry, we ate ham sandwiches slathered in Dijon mustard and washed them down with sips from a lukewarm can of Vernors.

As I grew older, my grandfather let me take the helm. I'd sit next to him, and he'd carefully transfer the lacquered tiller to my waiting hands. It seemed as if he were passing me a fragile family heirloom. "You're sailing the old *Charlest* now, boy," he'd say.

I zigzagged unevenly through the water and against the swirling currents and shifting wind. "I can't hold it steady."

"Steer two-seventy on the compass." He pointed to the number, and that's where I fixed my eyes. I tried to keep the orange arrow in the middle of the three digits. In light wind I did. In more dicey conditions though, I was all over the place, dizzy from focusing on the spinning innards of the compass.

One rather rough and windy day, my grandfather told me to look up, away from the nautical instruments. He told me to set my

eyes on the horizon. "But how can I steer the course?" I asked.
"You'll feel it."

"Feel it?" I grasped the tiller desperately while *Charlest II* was lifted and then dropped suddenly in the troughs between waves.

My grandfather put one of his hands on the tiller and pushed it away from his body; the sails luffed furiously in the stiff breeze. The boat stalled, and we were thrashed wildly like a piece of discarded jetsam. Then he set us back on course. After a short time, he pulled the tiller toward him, and we skidded off the sides of waves—awkwardly out of control. Now, he loosed his grip, took his hands away. He let me find the course, feel the boat in a groove, when the sails were taught; even in the stir of white-capped water, *Charlest II* hummed along smartly.

I had learned to steer the boat, to sail by the wind. My grandfather beamed his toothy smile.

As I remember it, we didn't talk much during that last afternoon on *Charlest II*. After we'd set the sails, he asked me to take the tiller. He sat in the corner of the cockpit with a cushion wedged behind his back, arms folded across his breast. When the sun crept lower, he put on a pair of oversized sunglasses the burnt-caramel color of root beer bottles. I had the sense that he was staring at me, watching as I guided his boat through the water.

As we always had, we talked sporadically about the lake and about the sleek crafts that shuttled in and out of the harbor. On that day though, I wanted to say more: I wanted to thank him for showing me how to tie bowlines and reef a main; for patiently sitting with me while I struggled at the helm. I wanted to tell him that I, too, felt a special connection to Lake Michigan; and I wanted to tell him I loved him—things I didn't know how to say. For me, it was like guessing the wind's velocity from the movements of a distant flag.

After we turned around and were headed back toward the harbor, I asked my grandfather if he would like to steer. "I'm OK," he answered.

"Would you like to, though?"

"Well, I guess I could steer her for a few minutes." He scooted over next to me. His shoulders sagged, his breaths short and labored. I knew he was tired.

Once he had his hand around the tiller, he seemed to brighten somewhat. He looked at the rolling dunes as if it were the first time he had ever seen them. "Those dunes sure are pretty with the sun on them like that," he said.

We approached the mouth of the channel. "I think you should take it," he said, gesturing at the tiller. "You take us in."

"Let's do it together." I started the engine and furled the jib, then sat down next to him, the same way he had with me so many years before. We both kept a hand on the tiller while we putted through the mouth of the channel: past Big Red and that great flapping American flag; past the waving beach grass, the rustling poplar trees. Past people who stood idly on the pier, gazing at *Charlest II*—the boat with a grandfather and his grandson at the same helm, finding their way together into the quiet harbor.

I come here sometimes to reflect, to say the things I never said to him. Words fall into waves that lap the shore like whispered secrets. Seagulls hunker behind driftwood, peering at me askance. There is a kind of truth in Lake Michigan, I think, a lucidity I haven't found in any other place. On this evening, as the sun tucks itself beneath the liquid horizon, and the sky is burnished in ethereal shades of pink and fuchsia, it almost seems as if my grandfather is out there. Perhaps he's telling me to ease or trim, to head up a little. Or perhaps, sometimes, he has a hand on the tiller, too, and I'm not steering the course alone.

The Pleasure Of Their Company

Frederic Sibley

Once, on our way to the west side of the state, we stopped at a biology station on Douglas Lake. Just the three of us. The spot where we pulled off the road had a little dock that jutted ten or twelve feet from shore. The two of them walked out and stood looking at the tufted clouds, not needing to talk, as mallards and mergansers paddled in the reeds. When they'd seen all they could, they turned to leave but couldn't help bumping into each other since the dock was so very narrow. The sweetest shyness touched them, and he joked to her, "Oh, it's you--," then took her hand to steady her step. In that one instant I glimpsed unmistakably the tender intent which brought me into this world.

Frederic Sibley has been writing poetry since he turned fifteen. His work has been published in England and Japan, as well as the United States, and it has won him several awards. He taught at the community-college level for many years.

In the Secret Hearts of Women

Roger Leslie

"Women, they're a mystery, son," my father would often say with a dismayed shake of his head. He loved my mother, always did. But, from my earliest years, such comments made me wonder what it was about women that men like my dad couldn't understand.

At home my parents cooperated to make everything in our family work. They taught us to be respectful, modeling polite behavior themselves. With their guidance, we studied hard in school. We honored our heritage. (Though none of us children spoke Polish, we still called some of our aunts *Ciocia* and sang *Sto Lat* on birthdays.) We developed disciplines that would make us successful.

In this staunch example, my father was very comfortable. Propriety, compassion, discipline, these were my father's traits. My mother lived them as well, but they were not who she was. The truth of my mother, the mystery of women that eluded my dad, seldom materialized at home. But once a year it burst alive with a radiant joy in the simplest of settings: my Auntie Angie's two-room cottage on the coast of Lake Huron.

Though the trip from Dearborn Heights to Port Austin was barely 100 miles straight up M-53, my mother was always nervous about making the drive. Anywhere else we went, my father drove. But something pushed Mom past her fear and inspired her to venture out of town with just my grandmother (we called her Baka), my sister, Judy; my little brother, Ray; and me.

Roger Leslie is a writer whose works include novels, history books, biographies, and motivational texts. Though he moved with his family to Houston when he was just fourteen, nearly all of his fiction is set in Michigan. Last year, Leslie's essay, *Wise Woman* appeared in Volume II of *Voices of Michigan.*

Usually around August 9th of every summer, we headed north in Mom's green AMC Hornet, stopping just once along the way for ice cream in Marlette. When we arrived in Port Austin, our first stop was always Chuck and Jane's Restaurant, where we ate thin pork chops and grew more eager about seeing the aunts and cousins waiting for us at the cottage.

When pulling into Auntie Angie's unpaved drive, my mother's excitement was as palpable as ours. Rocks, alternately painted orange and white, lined the forked driveway. The left path circled a garden in front of Auntie Angie and Uncle Eddie's spacious stone house, and the right led directly to the tiny cottage where we all stayed.

The sound of gravel crackling under our tires brought relatives out to welcome us. Aunt Arlene, my mother's younger cousin, stepped out to the covered porch. "Hi-iy!" Her sing-song greeting sounded like two syllables.

From around back of the house, petite Auntie Angie, Baka's older sister, walked delicately across her lawn, followed by her two excited poodles. Even working outside in the middle of summer, with dirty garden gloves on her hands, our wealthy great aunt was the picture of gentility. Every hair was in place, her slacks pressed and perfectly coordinated with her blouse. Perhaps because she never had children of her own, Auntie Angie always seemed thrilled when family visited. "Hi, honey," she would smile as she hugged each of us.

"Come on in," Arlene beamed. "Ma took the kids to the beach. They'll be back in a minute."

The cottage was divided into two main rooms, the kitchen on the left with a small bathroom behind it, and a bedroom on the right. As we children found places for our suitcases and sleeping bags in the bedroom, I could hear my mother's laughter resounding through the wall. At the time, I thought it was just the small space that made her laugh echo so richly. I soon discovered it was something more.

"Doll," Baka asked my mother when we were all gathered in the kitchen, "Where's my hanging bag?"

"What hanging bag? You just had this suitcase."

"No, all my clothes were in the hanging bag at my back door."

"I didn't get any—." My mother's face blanched. "Oh, no, Ma. We musta forgot it."

"We?!" Baka laughed, and everyone but my mother joined in.

"Ma, I'm so sorry. What are you gonna do without your clothes?" I knew this look on my mother's face. She often had it at home.

"Aaaaaa," Baka waved a carefree hand in the air. "I'm on vacation. What do I need?"

"But, Ma."

"Doll, I'll be fine. I'm with family."

With those words, my mother was transformed. She quit worrying, and immediately we—Mom, Judy, Ray, and I—were all free to enjoy our vacation.

That small cottage packed in more life and people than any space I'd ever seen. Throughout the afternoon, more and more relatives arrived. Ciocia Honey came back from the beach with Aunt Arlene's three small children. That evening, Ciocia Stas arrived with her two daughters, Nancy and Debbie.

"There's a fish fry at the VFW hall," Arlene offered near dinner time. "Let's all go there."

Auntie Angie hesitated. "Eddie wouldn't care for that. You go. I'll fix us something here when he gets home."

Like my father, Uncle Eddie was a powerful presence. He was a round, robust Russian with a booming voice that sprinkled expletives into every sentence.

A softly disappointed, "Well, Ang," was the only response anyone offered. There was no need to argue. Though she would have liked to go, Angie stayed back because of Uncle Eddie.

155

Thirteen of us piled into three cars. Except for my little brother Ray and my toddler cousin, Tommy, I was in exclusively female company.

Stories over dinner reminded me that my mother had grown up in Hamtramck in a household of nearly all women. Jaja and Babcia had immigrated to Detroit with their six daughters and built the family house, which Ciocia Stas now owned. After Jaja died, three generations of extended family lived there, usually at the same time.

I was captivated by the stories that the women began at dinner and continued as they played pinochle in the cottage that night. Men were seldom mentioned.

Apparently, while husbands worked at the factory or ran their corner bars, the sisters and daughters experienced the more memorable moments of their lives. As the evening in Port Austin wore on, the energy rose. We children were packed so tightly around the floor in our sleeping bags that we had to weave our way to the bathroom at night. Long past midnight, the melodious laughter of women wafted through the open windows, drowning out the waves of Lake Huron that crashed against the break wall of Auntie Angie's property.

Though she couldn't have gotten more than a few hours of sleep, my mother woke vibrant and happy the next morning. After breakfast, Ciocia Honey led us along a secret path to a private beach. There, my mother astounded me. On vacation anywhere else, she would have sat fully dressed under an umbrella, her hair protected from blowing sand by a tightly tied babushka. But in Port Austin, she raced with us along the shore. When Ciocia Honey showed us kids how to rub sand on our face to take care of our skin, Mom joined in, too. Most astounding of all, my mother, in her forties at the time, challenged Aunt Arlene to a handstand competition.

While everyone else laughed joyously, I was struck with curiosity. What was the magic of this experience that made my mother come alive as she never did at home?

That evening, many of us walked to town for dinner, then played putt-putt golf. Usually contentious, especially during games, Ray and I fell naturally into the harmony that everyone else seemed to be enjoying. Instead of vying for a winning score, we were captivated by the sweet innocence of our tiny cousin, Lisa. Still too young to count, Lisa hit the ball, and hit the ball, and hit the ball, then finally dragged it with her club until it dropped into the hole.

"Wow!" Aunt Arlene grabbed Lisa's hand and jumped up and down with her. "You got a hole-in-one." A little confused but no less joyful, Lisa looked around open-mouthed, then raced to the next green for more success.

In the end, we never did know who won. Frankly, it didn't matter. We were having too much fun to care.

Days always sped by during our Port Austin vacations. At some point, the kids would go to the one movie house in town while the women had drinks at Sportsman's Bar. Often, we went to the library where, every year, we checked out the same book about unusual people.

The old librarian always eyed us suspiciously as she stamped the due date card. "You know, you shouldn't make fun of these poor souls," she warned, just as my father would.

"Oh, no," Aunt Ar would placate her.

Then all the way home, Aunt Ar would find pictures of people, like the dog-faced lady, and make up stories that made us laugh till our sides hurt.

"Can you imagine, surprising your mom on prom night?" she'd say. "'Mom, I want to introduce you to my date,' and then you open the door to *her*." Aunt Ar pointed to the lady who looked like a schnauzer.

"Your mom would say, 'Oh, nice to meet you,' and your date would answer, 'Rrrrrrrrrhhhh.'"

Some years we rode to Bad Axe for their sidewalk sale. But at least once every summer Mom and Aunt Ar took us to the Port Austin dime store and let each of us buy a toy. Often, because

Auntie Angie's birthday fell some time around our visit, we would pick out a group present for her.

The only time we children were allowed into Auntie Angie's house was to celebrate her birthday. With its large picture window that looked out to the endless lake, her living room seemed enormous. Along one wall were porcelain figurines of women with delicately painted fingernails and stiff lace glued to the billowing hem of their dresses.

Much like our dog at home, we children were not permitted past the threshold of the living room. Instead, we stood around the kitchen table as Auntie Angie took a seat and Ciocia Stas carried in the birthday cake, candles already glowing.

As we sang "Happy Birthday" and "Sto Lat," I watched Auntie Angie's eyes gaze at each of us. Overcome with emotion, she gently stroked my cousin Laura's hair, and tears filled her eyes.

When we finished singing, Uncle Eddie noted Angie's rich emotion. "What the hell's wrong with you?" Even the youngest children knew Uncle Eddie's abrasive manner was unthreatening. Bewildered, he looked at us kids. "You know I worship that woman, but I don't understand her." Then he turned to her again. "What are you crying for? They said *happy* birthday. It's your birthday. Be happy."

At first, Auntie Angie was speechless. More tears fell. I looked around and all the women were teary. But it wasn't sad, like a funeral. It felt warmer than the sun outside, warmer than midnight conversations over pinochle in the cottage.

"Oh, Eddie," Angie finally said.

Uncle Eddie shrugged. "Blow out your candles, dammit, before the whole cake melts. This is a party."

He looked at me, the oldest boy there. "These women—crying at a happy occasion. I don't get it."

But that afternoon, I started to.

Each year, in some form, I saw the pattern in my mother continue. After she got us safely to Port Austin, her spirit seemed to meld into the atmosphere of the cottage. She talked more, laughed more. Her vocal inflections sounded increasingly similar to Ciocia Stas's and Ciocia Honey's. Within a day at Port Austin, my mother could do handstands on the beach. But when we completed our vacation and headed back home, I saw the transformation gradually reverse. The animation dimmed a little. Her shoulders tensed some. By the time we arrived home, she was all strict instruction and good example for her children.

I'm grateful for that stoic model. I know how hard my mother worked at being what she wanted us to become. But truthfully, I learned much more from the woman without secrets who came out to play every summer, if only briefly, in Port Austin. Through her, I solved the mystery and found my inspiration.

Torn From My Heart, A True Story

Elena Diamond-Young

Just because a child is not your flesh and blood doesn't mean your love for them is any less true, any less pure. I found that to be true on a cold November morning in 1995.

It was 7 a.m. as I sat on the edge of her bed. I gazed down into her face, trying to memorize every detail. Her face was so innocent. Her straight dark brown hair cascaded over her cheeks. The shadows of the morning angled across the room as the first light of the day started up the sky. I looked at her, this child of eight years, and hated the thought of disturbing her slumber. She was still and quiet. Her eyes fluttered occasionally, indicating that she was far away in a dream. I hoped it was a sweet one. Time seemed to stand still as I looked at her lying there.

> **Elena Diamond-Young** was born and reared in Kalamazoo, Michigan. Now divorced she and her son T. J., who is seven years old, left Texas in 1995 and returned home. Elena is now seeking a bachelor's degree in Sociology at Kalamazoo Valley Community College.

She did not know that she wouldn't be picking out something from her room for show and tell today, nor even going to school. She wouldn't get to say good-bye to the friends she had made, nor to the kind teacher that had been so helpful in making the difficult transition as a new student coming in to class in mid-semester. She didn't know yet that she would not be able to say good-bye to her aunts, uncles, and cousins that she had grown close to over the past months since we moved to Michigan. In a few minutes, her life would be drastically changed, and it was beyond her control and mine.

I sat on the bed, warm with her body, and watched my stepdaughter sleep. I thought back to when she became "my daughter" almost all at once. Some people have great difficulty gaining the trust and love of a stepchild. But for Jenna and me it was easy-- like honey, it flowed steady and sweet. She was my daughter, and no one could say she wasn't. People often remarked that we looked alike. I nursed her through the chicken pox. She laughed, thinking it was silly when I put socks on her hands to keep her from itching.

I taught her how to make a playhouse by stretching a sheet across two chairs and crawling inside. I remember how we played school and taught her the alphabet.

How proud I felt when her first-grade teacher called with praise for having her so well-prepared for school. Morning after morning we would pick out clothes together, until finally, she could do it all on her own. There were the secrets she would whisper to me. How I now wish I could remember what they were.

Once, her father, in a rage, threw away all her birthday cards and letters that she had been saving over the years. "You can't keep all this crap forever!" he cursed.

When he had soothed his anger with a beer and went back to tearing his car apart, I went into the kitchen and picked out all the cards and letters and tied them together with a ribbon. Later that day, I gave them back to the teary-eyed girl, telling her to keep them in a safe, secret place where no one could find them.

All these memories washed over me as I watched her sleeping. The morning was gaining, and I had put it off long enough.

I touched her shoulder and patted her gently. "Jenna, honey, wake up," I choked the words out.

She stirred and yawned, stretching her youthful limbs across the bed, kicking the covers down. "Morning, Mama," she said sleepily.

I braced my self again. "Sweetie, I have to tell you something important."

She sat up and rubbed her eyes, sweeping her straight hair from her face. "What, Mama?"

"Honey…" I paused, "your Daddy is here…from Texas."

It took a few seconds for the reality of it to set in.

"Daddy's here?" Then her eyes lit with joy.

"Yes, Daddy's here--to take you back with him."

Then, I could see it hit her. She knew right away what I was saying. Her father was here to take her back, and I was not going with them.

He had shown up with no notice, even though he had promised that she could stay through the school year, and that she would go back to him when he had a steady job and a place for them to live. Now he had come with no call to prepare either myself or his daughter. No time to pack all the things she had accumulated. The tears welled up in her eyes, and she threw herself into my arms and sobbed. We sat like that for a while, ten minutes or so, rocking back and forth. I reassured her that she would be fine, that all would be right.

I had asked him earlier if he would stay so she could say good-bye to her friends and family. He refused, saying he was pressed for time. I could not keep him from taking her. She was not my own. I didn't give birth to her. I wasn't really her mother. It tortured me knowing I had to send this bright little girl home with an angry, misogynistic, alcoholic. By law, I had no leg to stand on to stop it from happening.

When the crying had lessened, we went upstairs. She washed her face, and I helped her to get dressed, and brushed her hair, all for one last time. With clothes and toys crammed into garbage bags and stuffed into the trunk, we hugged and kissed.

She crawled, clutching her box of prized "secret girl things," into the back seat. I listened to the crunching of the tires on the gravel as they drove away.

The sun streamed down as morning settled in. A numbing wash came over me. An image of Jenna one year earlier flooded into my mind. We rocked, she on my lap, on a lazy summer afternoon, reading a Dr. Seuss book, when she said to me, "Mama,

I wish I had come out of your belly. Then I would be yours for real."

I laughed and said, "But honey, you are mine, and I love you no matter what."

She smiled and sighed, and as if she new what was to come, she said, "Yes, but if I came from YOUR belly, we could be together forever, no matter what."

Though we were never flesh and blood, there is not a moment when I don't feel as though there is a part of me missing, a part that had not *always* been there in the beginning, a part never grown from me, but torn from me with such pain, as if she had been my own.

The Great Leap

John Deckinga

With Asia Minor at his feet, Julius Caesar proclaimed, "I came, I saw, I conquered." I now understand exactly how he felt.

My wife Nancy and I were on a three-day vacation at Oaxtepec, a quiet oasis about two hours south of Mexico City. Oaxtepec has acres of green plants, beautiful flowers, grass, and plenty of sunshine: a great escape from Mexico City, where we were living at the time, with its miles of concrete and gallons of air pollution.

Oaxtepec's main attraction, besides the tranquility, is swimming. The resort has twenty-five wading, swimming, and diving pools. And so it was that I saw my personal Asia Minor: the ten-meter platform outside the dorm-like building where we were staying. The platform kept staring me in the face every time I went swimming or stepped out of the door of our lodging. It called to me: serene, imposing, frightening, and...well...high.

Ten meters--that's a little over thirty feet, not much when it's lying on the ground. After all, who ever heard of a ten-meter sprint? Or a ten-meter car race? It's only about ten long walking paces.

But pick that ten meters up off the ground with you on top of it, stand it upright, and watch the distance stretch. Add to that the Law of Inverse Shrinkage, and it becomes downright terrifying.

In layperson's terminology, the Law of Inverse Shrinkage states that the size of a diving pool shrinks by the square of the

> **John Deckinga**, originally from Chicago, lived for nearly fourteen years in Bolivia and Mexico. The influence of Latin America can be seen in much of his writing. John survived the Great Leap to come to northern Michigan, where he now does his writing safely on terra firma.

height of the board or platform. That means, when you're way up there on a ten-meter platform, you're sure to miss the pool.

Now Olympic divers defy the Law of I.S. They are able to flit and twirl from ten-meter platforms, and then slip neatly into the waiting pool, without missing. But their maneuvers fall into the realm of fantasy, or the nearly miraculous. What I'm talking about are strictly low-level, amateur ten-meter leapers, not professional, or near professional, divers.

And so, in spite of the odds against my surviving a ten-meter jump according to the Law of I.S., I determined--from the security of my prone position on a soft towel on terra firma--that I would leap from that platform.

With my neck craned, during the course of the day, I observed people jump from that platform, and I drew two conclusions. The first was that no matter how high that platform seemed, or how much the Law of Inverse Shrinkage applied, the jumpers always survived. They whoomped and voomped and shwoomped into the water, but they always floated, relatively unhurt, to the surface.

The second conclusion was that the prospective jumpers always seemed to have trouble if they walked to the end of the platform and stopped. That was obviously a mistake, as I saw it, because, inevitably, it resulted in a long period of fierce negotiating with themselves. In some cases, the person finally jumped; but in others, the negotiations resulted in defeat, and the person sheepishly made his or her way back down the ladder. In either case, it resulted in prolonged agony there at the edge of space, with cowardly "friends" down below egging them on, while the person's own mind split in two: one half urging, "Do it!" and the other half screaming, "DON'T YOU DARE, YOU IDIOT!"

Parenthetically, I want to clarify one thing. I was not in any way influenced by a skinny pre-teenage boy, who, after agonizing argumentation with himself at the edge of the platform, and the coaxing of friends below, did jump off that ten-meter platform. No, no, that had nothing whatsoever to do with shaming me into my self-destructive, stupid decision to repeat his performance. What that young man did was his own decision. The little show-off.

Anyway, back to my two observations. I concluded that I probably would survive the jump, but if I stopped at the end of the platform, I would never go off. When my time came, I had to say a simple "Geronimo" and keep on walking.

As part of my buildup and training strategy, I decided to jump off the five-meter platform three times before attempting the ten-meter platform. That would give me practice in keeping my arms down by my side, so they wouldn't smack the water and perhaps disintegrate or separate from my body. Also, I could practice walking off the end without stopping. And the five-meter platform would give me something of a feel for the BIG ONE.

As I look back on it now (from this hospital bed. No, just kidding...really), going off that five-meter platform was a remarkable feat in itself, since I had never jumped off a five-meter platform before in my life. But I did go off, not three times, but five or six, because I ran into problems.

First, my arms had, as it were, a mind of their own, and would not heel to my command. They went off in their own directions.

Second, was a major flaw in my strategy, and something which threatened my whole plan. I found it impossible to simply walk off the end of the platform and still keep my balance. I had to stop at the end for at least a split second to bring my feet together, get my balance, and then step off the end. That meant, no matter what, there would be a crisis at the end of the ten-meter platform where I would face the screaming part of my mind and be sorely tempted to begin negotiating with it.

Jumping off the five-meter platform, I also noticed that I hit the water very hard. Running some crude calculations through my frenzied mind, I figured that off the ten-meter platform I would hit at least twice as hard, and my precious body would surely vaporize.

But I forced myself to concentrate on the one-hundred percent survival rate that I had observed earlier in the day. Theoretically at least, I would survive.

Fortunately, at this time of day--late in the evening--there weren't many people using the platforms, so I could train at my own pace and not be pressured by the performance or laughter of others. Finally the big moment came. I started climbing the same steps I had been climbing during my training period. But this time, at the halfway point--the five-meter platform--I kept on climbing, and made my shaky way into the ionosphere. (Oh no, I had overlooked oxygen depletion. Would I simply pass out up there and have to be carried down? Or worse yet, would I faint and fall to my death into the pool, or, according to the Law of Inverse Shrinkage, outside the pool?)

I wouldn't say that I clung to the handrail, exactly. Let's just say that I held onto it, very firmly, so it wouldn't blow away. The view at the top was lonely and breathtaking. I felt like an astronaut or a mountain climber. Remarkably, I did not faint.

I paused for only a moment. The critical seconds were upon me. I walked resolutely to the end of the platform, stopped to put my feet together, looked down into the jaws of death, and noted that I would surely miss the pool. As that second part of my mind began to cry out in agony, "NO, NO, NO!" I stepped out into space.

The trip down was rather uneventful, except for my stomach slamming against the inside top of my skull. About halfway down, I commented to myself that I still had halfway to go. I let out a helpless whimper and continued on my way.

I must have hit the water somewhere near the speed of sound, but I hit it more or less upright, although my arms were slightly awry, and I seem to remember surviving the impact. However, for scientific research purposes, I can't recall whether I hit with a whoomp, a voomp, or a shwoomp.

All that was eclipsed by a great sense of relief that the ordeal was over, and by the sense of accomplishment that I had conquered not just the ten-meter platform, but Fear itself.

Although Nancy was the only person applauding as I popped to the surface and drifted to the edge of the diving pool, in my mind, a crowd of thousands had risen to their feet and were wildly cheering my triumph.

I bowed to their applause.

The Old Jennings Place

Helen Sanecki

The fences are down. Their posts rotted away by the elements and time. Laid low by howling winds and banks of drifting snow, the falling posts took the fence lines down with them. Between the squares of broken, rusting wires grow tall grasses and weeds alongside thorny blackberry bushes and wild apple trees. Once these fences guarded fields of golden grain – wheat, oats, rye, and barley—gently waving in the northern breeze; fields of corn, clover, and alfalfa; orchards and gardens. No longer checked and repaired every Spring, the fences lie where they fall.

The fields seed themselves. Each season brings its own potpourri of growing plants. Spring bursts forth in various shades of green, then sprinkles the fields with bright yellow dandelions. Summer overflows with lacey white wild carrot intermingled with black-eyed susans and white daisies. Wild strawberry vines creep along the sunny hillsides. Goldenrod dominates the late summer, and burdock and thistle grow purple blooms, the size of which you have never seen. When the milkweed pods begin to burst and shed their silky down seeds, summer is coming to an end. A short while, and the whole landscape is arrayed in brilliant shades of yellow, orange and red;

Helen Sanecki, a farmer's daughter who returned to the family farm in Harrisville after living in the Detroit area for over forty years, is retired from the Detroit School system where she worked for thirty one years, the last seventeen as a high school counselor. She has been published in the *Michigan History Magazine* and won second-place in the Thunder Bay Literary Conference Writers Competition in 1990.

then, all is stripped by the winds and the seeds scattered over the fields.   Spring brings all to life again.

The winding, rippling stream is gone.   The springs ran dry, leaving a stony path among the evergreens.   Huge stone bolders lie in dried mud holes.   No longer do brookies or rainbow swim under the wooden bridge.   No ducks nest in marshes along the stream nor do they swim in its waters with their broods of fuzzy yellow ducklings.   No cattle line up at the banks for a drink of clear cool water.   Ferns cover the cow paths, some with fronds shoulder high. The stately elms, which grew throughout the pasture, have all fallen prey to Dutch elm disease.   Their gray trunks hover over the land like giant ghosts.   Woodpeckers chip away at the rotting wood, some searching for insects, others, cutting out holes large enough to nest their young.

The barns stand empty, the roofs leaking, the windows broken.   Under the eaves, swallows tend their young, undisturbed. The odor of molding hay permeates the whole area.   In the cattle barn, the stalls are falling apart.   An old straw hat lies in one of the mangers; another holds two milking stools.   The cream separator stands in the milk room, just as it was left when the last pail of milk was run through for cream.   A large white enamel pan, where cats lined up for warm milk every morning and evening, lies upside down near the separator.   In the horse barn, a set of harnesses still hangs on the wall and a pitch fork stands in the corner near the big wooden door.   Elederberry bushes hide the door to the hen house and animal burrows, from mice to woodchucks, can be seen everywhere.

The house stands on its hilly pedestal.   Its cedar siding, once the white of freshly fallen snow, has turned a weather-beaten dingy gray.   The windows, their shades torn, are covered with dust and grime, and spiders spin silvery threads across the threshold. Hollyhocks crowd around the picket fence.   Wild grasses over-run the walkways.   Near the entrance gate stands a huge gray stone with faint traces of once big black letters spelling out ROBERT JENNINGS.   The old homestead stands forlorn and haunting; yet, when evening comes, and the sun is moving toward the hills, the windows of the old house capture and reflect the golden rays of the setting sun, returning to the old gray house some of its inviting warmth of former days – a certain glow, like the promise of another tomorrow, another generation.

Voices of Michigan

Depression Ice

Marty Z

The iceman contributed to the welfare and comfort of people during the period of the Depression. Our family was a part of this effort.

During the Depression, our family owned a produce farm. I was also involved with a canning factory, making thirty-five cents an hour. Top wages at the time!

One day our local banker excitedly approached my father and proposed that we start an ice business. He said Dad had the manpower of six sons to do this type of work, and to make a good living. The banker felt that competition was needed in the local ice business, because the price was too high, and the service was bad.

And so, we got to work and built a huge, barn-like shelter with insulated, double walls, which we filled with wood sawdust. We had an ingenious brother, Frank, who made a circle saw, powered by a Ford Model A motor. The best description of this machine is that it was like a self-propelled, powerful lawnmower. This was used to mark the ice.

> **Marty Z** was born in 1918. He is a retired chief with two daughters and a son, and is happily married to Mary. In describing this writing, Martin stated, "My visits to Michigan to see my daughter and her family at their hand-built log home on Lake Charlevoix have motivated me to reflect and share my thoughts about this period of my life."

The harvesting of the ice took place on a crystal clear, artesian-fed lake. This man-made lake was called "Number Two Clayhole." (It got its name from the clay which was used to manufacture building bricks.)

In the winter, when the lake was frozen, we would take my brother's invention and mark the ice about six inches deep. We used a hand saw to separate the quantity we wanted from the field, before floating the ice, directed by the men, using long-handled ice hooks, down the channel. From there the blocks would go up the conveyor belt, to the platform, and onto the trucks, ready to deliver their cargo to the ice house which held some 5000 cakes of ice, each of them weighing about 500 pounds. These cakes of ice were covered with sawdust through the winter and into the summer, to hold them through the summer.

Our work schedule was from five in the morning until eight at night. At that time, people were begging for work. We hired eight to ten people at thirty-five cents per hour - the best rate we could afford. Everyone appreciated the work, and we got along lovely, especially because of my mother and father's generosity.

My dad came to the United States from Germany at the turn of the century, at age sixteen. His family moved to an area North, where Germans were not welcome. Their home was burned down, and they moved to a community of German, Polish and Scandinavian descent. My father was a forgiving individual. He and my mother loved their new area, because everyone got along beautifully.

Their life was spent taking care of their family and others around them. During the Depression, people came off the railroad train which was 200 feet from our house. Whole families would be looking for food, water or work. I never saw my parents turn down anyone for food, and we had a little bunkhouse where they could stay the night. Similarly, in the ice business, my father's business sense (which was very good) often was superceded by his generosity. He had a stack of customer's bad checks that were six inches high. He forgave each one of them saying, "Maybe they will pay me some day." Lots of them never did.

Mother was a good provider, bookkeeper and cook, and she kept the family together. She would buy 100 pound bags of flour for her own bakery work of bread and rolls. Because our family was a family of twelve, she did a lot of canning of fruits and vegetables. My twin sister and two younger sisters were helpful to Mother around the house and in the fields. We ate most of our meals at home or grabbed a sandwich on the ice route. Six sons could cause a big commotion, and mother was the peacemaker. She had the most loveable temperament of anyone you could know.

One time during a very dry period, Mother faithfully went to water the pigs. She used a bucket that had contained red lead paint, and poisoned everyone one of them. She always felt bad about that. And mother never swore, except the time she was going to treat the family to a pineapple upside-down cake. She brought it from the oven to the serving table, and it flipped upside down, onto the floor! She said a couple of naughty words. We all had to laugh.

In the business, Father went along as one of the boys, but insisted upon fine English and would allow no profanity with his crew. He was talented in his own way, and his management was good, always working hard to make the ice venture into a profitable business.

In what little free time he had, Father was interested in good music. We had a phonograph, the crank type. He bought us one of the best radios we could have at the time. So we got the news of the five little girls born in Canada and Lindy's flight over the Atlantic, which held a special interest to my father who had met him.

But there was little time for that. The ice business was a hectic way of life. How the rotary phone would ring! Temperatures in the summer were in the hundreds. "Please bring more ice to the tavern, because the beer is getting warm, and the unemployed are complaining." (At that time you could buy ten ounces of beer for five cents.) The homes would receive ice two to three times a week at the price of two-and-a-half or three dollars a month. "Could you please bring more ice. The milk is starting to curdle." And on it went, for fifteen years.

The ending of our ice business was the introduction of electric refrigeration and modern methods of food preservation. Three of the boys went into the service, and we were all glad to get out of the business. No more harvesting ice at ten below zero and working fifteen hours a day, delivering ice in the hot summer months.

Happy memories, but a relief to get rid of it.

The Forgotten Highway

Therese Malmberg

The Forgotten Highway starts at the very tip of the Keweenaw Peninsula, the northernmost point in Michigan, thrusting into Lake Superior like a rhino's horn piercing the sky. Rising out of the base of the Upper Peninsula, it is a land largely forgotten by the rest of the world. Maps—when they bother to show it at all—frequently show it as part of Wisconsin, or even Canada. Its people—popularly called Yoopers—are a clannish, fiercely independent folk, who resent being bound to Lansing (and sometimes to Washington, D.C., as well). I am but one of its many children in exile, cast forth because there were no jobs, and no Jew ever yearned for Jerusalem, or Muslim for Mecca, the way the Keweenaw exiles are homesick for their cold northern land.

> **Therese Malmberg** was born in 1956 in Marquette and now lives in Mattawan. She enjoys writing about travel and history. Her entry, *The Forgotten Highway*, is an adaptation of chapter one from a book she is currently working on about U.S. Highway 41.

Although I now live in the bottom corner of the western Lower Peninsula, like many other exiles, I keep in touch with my roots by making the long two-day journey North whenever possible. Part of this ritual includes visiting Copper Harbor, a hamlet of some fifty year-round residents clustered around a horseshoe-shaped lagoon at the very tip of the Keweenaw, and this is where my story begins.

If you follow the pavement East a mile or so out of town, you will come to a single-lane, blacktop circle in a tiny clearing in the woods. In the center of the circle there is a large wooden sign bearing a lime-green map of the Eastern United States and the legend:

THE BEGINNING OF US 41

Early Indian footpaths became the trails for explorers, missionaries and fur traders who came to carve out homes in Michigan's wilderness. The early settlers began to widen and improve these trails which became the majority of Michigan's primary highway system.

US 41 starts its southbound journey here, crossing eight states which include Michigan, Wisconsin, Illinois, Indiana, Kentucky, Tennessee, Georgia, and ending in Miami, Florida, a distance of 1,990 miles.

How well I know that road! It holds many memories for me: two-lane, scenic, winding through seemingly endless forest, breaking out into the sunlight of hayfields and cow pastures, running along Lake Superior's rocky shore, past ghost towns that had once been bustling, and small cities that had hopes their future would be every bit as glorious as their past. What I did not know, however, was that U.S. 41 had a past equally as exciting, that beyond the Upper Peninsula, it had been as important as the much more celebrated Route 66. It was a chance remark made by a man in Evansville, Indiana—"You're traveling the Dixie Bee!"—that made me take another look at this road.

The history of this part of U.S. 41 goes back to 1837 when Michigan became a state. Seven hundred miles from the Keweenaw, war was about to break out between Michigan and Ohio over the Toledo Strip, when Washington, D.C., seeking to avoid bloodshed, stepped in. The disputed area was awarded to Ohio, while Michigan received the northern peninsula (at that time belonging to Wisconsin) in compensation.

The people of Michigan were outraged, viewing the Upper Peninsula in much the same light as the Alaska Purchase would be viewed several decades later. They sang scornful songs about "that poor frozen country beyond Lake Michigan." (What Wisconsin thought is never mentioned in Michigan history books.) However, since Michiganders were saddled with this wasteland, they decided to survey it.

To everyone's surprise, in 1841 geologist Douglass Houghton reported that the region, far from being a wasteland, was rich in copper and other minerals. His warning that it also had the potential to become the ruin of hundreds, went unheeded. Houghton's reports set off a stampede. According to Keweenaw lore, when Horace Greeley uttered the famous words of John Soule, "Go West, young man," it was to Michigan's copper district that he referred. From all over war and famine-torn Europe, immigrants rushed to Upper Michigan, making it a crucible of many diverse northern and eastern European nationalities. It was from this mixture that the Upper Peninsula's unique dialect evolved: part Canadian, part Scandinavian, and part something unidentifiable.

In 1844, the federal government (fearing Indian attacks on the fortune-seekers pouring into the "Copper Country") built Fort Wilkins on the banks of Lake Fanny Hooe just outside Copper Harbor. (Now, a state park, its restored palisade is the first and last sight that greets visitors to the northern end of the highway.) Its soldiers did not consider being posted there as a particularly desirable assignment. Who wanted to be stuck in a backwater of black flies and mosquitoes and six-foot snow banks when the Mexican War was threatening to break out at any moment? It didn't help that Fanny Hooe, the fort commander's sister-in-law, disappeared one spring day in 1846, when she took her washing down to the lake which now bears her name. Other stories are told of soldiers bound for the fort, who deserted, en route, while others tried, unsuccessfully, to buy substitutes for themselves. As for the Indians, their main hunting grounds lay outside the Keweenaw (the name, in fact, meant "the place we go around"). It turned out that the fort was largely unnecessary.

Nevertheless, in the 1850's, two enterprising civilians, Samuel W. Hill and Ed Hulbert, applied for, and were granted, a contract to build a military road from Copper Harbor to Green Bay, Wisconsin. The Military Road, though it can be said to have been a forerunner of U.S. 41, did not follow the same route as today's highway. This is partly because Hill and his partner stipulated they were to be paid in land, instead of cash; the government agreed, insisting that the land had to be within three miles of the road. Hill and Hulbert then went around and selected what they thought to be the most promising mining sites, and built the road to connect them. Moreover, they subcontracted sections out to men like Dan Brockway, a Copper Harbor hotel owner who gave his name to the "mountain" overlooking the harbor. This freed Hill and Hulbert for more time mining. The end result was described as a road that "squirmed something akin to a reptile in the grass."

Despite its name, the Military Road was never used as such. Rather, it served as an immigrant trail and bootlegging route (a role the later U.S. 41 expanded to perfection), and gradually fell into disuse, as other roads were built. Only scattered bits and pieces now remain throughout the U.P. and northern Wisconsin.

Sam Hill's name, though, lasted longer than his road. As John Bartlow Martin put it in *Call It North Country*: "His propensity for profanity was legendary. His neighbors, retelling his tall tales in polite society, substituted 'Sam Hill' for the more lurid phrases, and Hill's fame spread far beyond the Copper Country; he became, indeed, a part of the American language as mule-skinners roared: 'What the Sam Hill!' all the way from Bent's Fort to Manassas Junction."

Copper Harbor, back then, was a far cry from today's sleepy tourist town. Copper Harbor was populated with saloons and boardinghouses where three shifts of miners often slept in the same dirty sheets, because there was no time for the overworked women who ran the boardinghouses to change and wash the sheets. The miners would not recognize it now: just another stop on the Lake Superior Circle Tour, gateway to Isle Royale National Park: gift shops and restaurants and motels.

At least Copper Harbor still is a town, unlike many of the communities that had formed like nodes of copper along the spine of the peninsula. Some are now ghost towns. Others, like Mandan, Delaware, Central, Phoenix, Cliff, Ahmeek, Allouez, Phillipsville,

Kearsarge, and Centennial, just hang on. If the truth be known, these forgotten towns on U.S. 41, in their peak years, were as rowdy or even rowdier than anything the so-called Wild West had to offer: It was fists, rather than guns, that settled disputes. Up on Quincy Hill, just above Hancock, things were so wild that the newspapers officially dubbed the district "Helltown," according to Clarence J. Monette's 1975 booklet on Copper Country names and places. As late as August 1919, Monette said, the situation became so serious that the people living there "were forced to petition their supervisor to take action to stop the lawlessness," and "many of the older residents remember when Helltown was a personification of the Wild West." The tourists in their Winnebagos don't know this, and neither does Hollywood; perhaps it is better this way.

From Copper Harbor, U.S. 41 turns South to enter a twenty-mile long tunnel of aspen and birch at the base of Brockway Mountain. These "little mountains" which surround the highway are the remains of ancient volcanoes, their fire long since solidified into the abundant red metal that gave the Copper Country its name. Although history books give more attention to California's Gold Rush, it was this copper that was actually far more important to the nation's economy. They say around here: "Our copper was the 'silica chip' (sic) of the Industrial Revolution."

Tradition says that Horace Greeley visited the peninsula in 1856 to see how his investment in the Delaware Mine was faring. When he reached Eagle River, he almost drowned trying to get off his boat, and ended up leaving, without ever seeing the mine. A hill to the southeast of Delaware—on which two towns now reside—still bears his name. Old Delaware consists of a row of decaying, identical two-story frame houses (the kind found in every Upper Peninsula mining town) along the highway not far from the mine. These had been abandoned long before the Depression. New Delaware is just down the road, a tiny hamlet of slightly newer homes.

"We aren't offering guided tours right now," the young woman at the cash register of the Delaware Mine explained, when I stopped in, "but you are welcome to tour the mine on your own." She pointed to a row of yellow miners' hats hanging by the back door. "Just take a hard hat with you. That way we know someone's down there. We count 'em at the end of the day, before we lock the mine up for the night." I noticed that her voice lacked the distinctive lilt of the native-born Yooper, so I asked her where she was from. It turned out that she was from the Lower Peninsula, and had moved North to get away from its crime and congestion. "It's so much more pleasant here," she said.

I could not agree with her more. There seems to be no neutral ground as far as tourists' feelings for the Upper Peninsula go—they either love it or hate it. The ones that hate it say it is too remote and the people too clannish; these usually do not return. To the ones who love the Upper Peninsula, it is heaven.

Most visitors, however, only see the Upper Peninsula during the summer. In the winter, it is another place entirely. Delaware, with an average annual snowfall of two hundred inches, is the "Snow Capital of the Midwest." Every winter its residents have a festival in honor of Heikki Lunta, the Finnish God of Snow, who rewarded them in 1978 with a record snowfall of 390.4 inches. In commemoration of this event, an enormous red thermometer was placed on the highway just south of Delaware.

One summer, two motorcyclists from New England were heading North on U.S. 41 when they spotted the red thermometer sign. "Hey look," one signaled, "a United Way pole—check it out! What's a United Way sign doing way out here in the sticks?"

"That's not a United Way sign!" exclaimed his companion as they halted and were craning their necks to read the top. "That's a snowfall record sign—says they get thirty feet of snow a year here. THIRTY FEET OF SNOW! How do people live here in the winter?" They would have been even more astonished to learn that Upper Peninsula winters are a matter of pride.

Up here, people don't shovel their sidewalks; they simply

roll out wooden ones with steps leading down to the road. Once, I climbed up the snow bank to pose next to the green-and-white sign announcing Florida, a town located just off U.S. 41 on the east side of Laurium. I had no trouble touching the eleven-foot high sign, though I barely stand five feet in regular shoes; and that was not a particularly severe winter. Florida in winter is worth seeing, if only for the sight of snow. But you will look in vain to find Florida on the state highway map; not even DeLorme's meticulously researched atlas shows it, though it shows countless other eye-blink towns. I never did learn how Florida got its name, apart from the fact that it was named after a long-defunct mine.

"Most will not understand this," wrote a local journalist, describing U.S. 41 in winter, "but it's a quirky romance over its miles for those who have chosen to live here." The winter highway, "caressed with less than gentle curves and struggling along through the land's wilder parts" is "an icy ribbon, smooth but scrubbed lightly with sand . . . U.S. 41 is carved out of ice, with the whitest, widest, wildest medians you'll ever see."

In its earliest years, (the road that was to become U.S. 41 was built in 1919) the highway was not plowed, but allowed to drift shut, adding to the Keweenaw's isolation. Some sections were rolled with a horse-drawn roller composed of two steel cylinders in diameter five to six feet.

Now, of course, the highways of the Keweenaw are kept open year round, often in conditions that would cause their downstate counterparts to be closed. When the road crews can not get out with their giant Sno-go's that throw snow higher than a house, things are bad indeed. Then people just sit back and wait. In a few hours the wind will die down and the plows will be back at work clearing the roads. "We keep our roads cleaner than you do downstate," my father told me, and it is true.

Traveling South down the center of the peninsula, I pass through familiar towns and landmarks that I know like the back of my hand. There is the long rocky escarpment paralleling the highway at Cliff, where a prospector literally fell onto the mother lode. At Phillipsville there is the antique shop (formerly a saloon and whorehouse) with "THE LAST PLACE ON EARTH" sign in large white letters standing boldly against the red brick wall. The word "ANTIQUES" is hidden by a group of trees, so the northbound traveler, rounding the curve and starting down the low rise into Phillipsville, can only see "THE LAST PLACE ON EARTH." By that time, that is exactly where most people feel they are.

Some years ago two Michigan Tech students put a mileage sign four miles south of Houghton on U.S. 41 which read "**End of Earth 2, Houghton** 4." It remained until the authorities made them take it down. "Can't be confusing the poor tourists," they said.

"It's not the end of the world," said my aunt, who was living in Chassell at the time, "but you can see it from here."

Then there are the historic red sandstone buildings of Calumet, full of magnificent churches whose spires compete with each other to reach the sky.

Calumet received its start when Ed Hulbert, surveying his and Sam Hill's meandering road--at that time reaching the halfway point down the peninsula--received word that some pigs had escaped from Billy Royal's tavern, and would he help look for them? Hulbert stopped work and joined the search. Royal's pigs were discovered rooting around in a nearby pit, which, when the men took a closer look, turned out not to be a natural depression, but a man-made one: a mine, dug out of a copper-bearing rock the Cornish miners called puddingstone. It had obviously been deserted for many years. The question was, who had dug it?

All over the Keweenaw, and also on Isle Royale, similar pits were being found, some with crude tools left in them, as if the miners had simply left for a break and were coming back soon. Other pits, carefully propped up with logs, held great masses of copper weighing several tons. Carbon testing later dated some of the tools to 2,000 B.C. Yet apart from the pits and the tools, no other traces of these mysterious people have yet been found--no campsites, burial grounds or villages. They simply vanished along with the copper. Only Lake Superior and the wilderness know who they were and where they went.

Ed Hulbert did not become rich from his find. Because he needed capital to develop the new mine, he went to Boston where he persuaded Quincy Adams Shaw, a Boston Brahmin, if there ever was one, to invest in his company. Shaw ended up controlling most of the stock, and eventually ousted Hulbert, in favor of his brother-in-law, Alexander Agassiz, son of the famed naturalist Louis Agassiz, and a naturalist in his own right.

During the 1860's, and afterwards, Agassiz built the Calumet and Hecla Mine (C & H) into a company that set the standard for all other Keweenaw mines. The "Benevolent Octopus," as the C & H was nicknamed, made Calumet a prosperous community of sixty thousand. In addition to the sandstone buildings, and magnificent church steeples, Calumet soon featured paved and lighted streets, a streetcar line linking it to the twin cities of Houghton and Hancock, and the first phone system in Michigan. When Calumet was faced with a surplus of funds in its treasury, it built an elaborate red sandstone opera house. Soon the biggest names in entertainment—Jenny Lind, John Phillip Sousa, and others—passed up concert dates elsewhere to perform at the opera house. A rumor even went around that the state capitol was about to be moved from Lansing to Calumet! In only a few short years, "that poor frozen country" had gone from neglected backwater, to Michigan's fastest-growing region.

Most people were fairly satisfied with C & H's paternalism, but there was a significant minority whose discontent was played upon by "outside" labor organizers. The Socialists and Communists were especially active. The mine owners and bosses did not bother to distinguish among the different groups. To them, *anyone* advocating a union was a troublemaker. In 1913, the smoldering unrest on the copper range blew up into a full-scale strike against

Calumet and Hecla. The strike was sparked by the company's decision to switch to a new one-man drill that the miners considered dangerous. It was not long before violence broke out, fanned by ethnic and religious rivalries. The entire Michigan National Guard was called to Calumet in an attempt to restore order.

To many people, the central figure of the strike is not Clarence Darrow (who came to Calumet to defend the striking miners). Nor is the central figure Bill Moyers, president of the Western Federation of Miners. A young woman the miners called "Joan of Arc" is the central figure. The wife of a miner, Annie Clemenc had long been interested in labor issues. When the strike began, she quickly stepped into the role of leader, marching through the streets of Calumet. At the head of the strikers' Sunday parades, she carried the American flag. The rest of the week she and other women could be found at the mines berating the "scabs" that dared to cross the picket line. Annie was not one to mince words. Once, during a demonstration, she issued a ringing challenge to the Guardsmen who were threatening her: "If this flag won't protect me, then I will die with it!" The Guardsmen stepped back.

As Christmas approached that year, Calumet was still bitterly divided. There was little money to spend on Christmas, due to the strike, but Annie, and the other women, determined that the children would still have their celebration. She and other women took time out from their picketing and parading to organize a holiday program. That Christmas Eve, seven hundred people, mostly strikers and their families, packed Italian Hall for the festivities.

What happened next sparked a controversy that ripped Calumet apart even more, and it is a controversy that has never been resolved. The party was well underway when an unknown man appeared in the hall and shouted, "FIRE!" In the rush for the doors, it was forgotten that they opened inward. The rumor swept through the panicked crowd that they had been deliberately locked, adding to the terror and confusion. By the time rescuers arrived, seventy-three people, mostly children, had been trampled to death. There had been no fire.

The strikers blamed the Citizens' Alliance, a group that had opposed the strike; the Alliance, in turn, denied the charge and suggested that one of the strikers might be responsible. A massive search began for the culprit. He was never found.

Eighty years later, a man phoned the Houghton *Daily Mining Gazette* claiming to have the truth about what happened at Italian Hall. A reporter spoke to him, and after promising him anonymity, heard the following story. The night of the "fire" a young man had been drinking in the bar below the hall before going upstairs and giving the false alarm. Afterwards, stricken with remorse, he helped carry the bodies out and dig their graves. For years afterwards, he tried to atone for his deed by helping others whenever he could. Finally, his burden of guilt became too much, and he went to the police. "It was meant as a prank," the then middle-aged man sobbed, adding that he had experienced nightmares ever since. After some discussion, the witnesses to his confession decided, for the safety of the confessor's family, as well as his own, not to reveal his identity. He had suffered enough, they felt, and with that the case was quietly closed.

The mysterious caller, talking to the reporter, said that the man had died years ago, and that all the witnesses to the confession were now dead except for him. He was getting on in years and was not expected to live much longer, which is why he made the call. After his death, he hinted, the identity of the man who cried, "Fire!" would be revealed. The paper printed the story as the man told it, adding only that this was merely a possible answer to the questions surrounding the Italian Hall tragedy. So much time had elapsed that the truth would probably never be known. It was better to let the matter rest.

But it would never be forgotten.

In the end, the miners won the strike, but it was a hollow victory. The situation was the same as that described by Bob Dylan in "North Country Blues": The Eastern mine owners claimed they were paying too much for ore they considered not worth digging, and turned to South America "where the miners work almost for nuthin'."

One by one, beginning in the Depression, the mines shut down. Even giant Calumet and Hecla was no more. Calumet's population dwindled as the shaft houses rusted among the hills, and the tunnels filled up with water. The roofs and walls of the stamp mills and smelters caved in, leaving a bombed-out appearance. The once-prosperous Keweenaw began to rival Appalachia—but without Appalachia's publicity.

Poet Gus Linja summed it up well: "To most people around here," he told me, "U.S. 41 was known mainly as the route the immigrants came in on. After the mines closed down, it became the road that took their children away."

I was one of them.

The Rain Tent

Sheri Radel

First of all, let me say I am not the least bit superstitious. I love black cats---except when they shed on white furniture. If I break a mirror, I don't worry about seven years of bad luck. I just dread cleaning up the broken glass. If the shortest path to somewhere happens to take me under a ladder, so be it. But, every once in awhile a pattern of events takes place that seems...shall we say, "unusual?"

My story begins back in the early 70's, when my husband and I were newlyweds. We didn't have much money, but we shared a great love of the outdoors. Like a lot of people in Michigan, or the rest of the country for that matter, we loved camping. In fact, camping equipment was at the top of our wedding gift wish list. While most engaged couples of that time registered fine china and silver patterns, we registered for sporting goods. And that's just how we got our first tent.

> **Sheri Radel** has called Michigan her home for almost thirty years. She lives in Muskegon with her husband and son. A former retail sales manager, Sheri now designs cakes and invitations.

It was a nine by nine umbrella tent. Eighty-one square feet of floor space. It sounds big enough for two people, doesn't it? But what you don't realize is the nine by nine is measured at the base of the tent. So, if you're one inch tall, you've got it made. But, for real people, the actual area in which to stand upright is really two by two in the center of the tent. So, it was cozy when we were newlyweds, but a bit cramped when we had been married a few months. For the sake of our marriage, it was time to look for something a little bigger.

The first day we checked the classifieds, there it was: the answer to our dreams. "A slightly used, in good condition, ten by twelve canvas tent." That meant thirty-nine more square feet of space. Room for two people to stand at the same time—better still, maybe even turn around at the same time. We knew we had to have this tent. So we called and made arrangements to see it.

Sure enough, it appeared the ad was accurate. The couple selling the tent showed us a picture of it on the outside of the box. They had tried to stuff it back into the carton, which is impossible, everyone knows, once the box has left the factory. What we could see of the tent, hanging out of the box, looked in good condition.

We didn't ask, but they explained that they had decided to "trade up" to a camper. And we didn't ask, but they offered to reduce the already low price by ten dollars. We should have seen the signs, but we didn't, not even when backing out of their driveway (with the tent safely loaded in our trunk). We noticed the family through their picture window. They had their arms around each other and were jumping up and down. They looked really happy. We smiled at each other thinking they must have really needed the extra cash.

Our first big outing with the tent was a belated honeymoon trip to Yellowstone in October. Tent campers aren't exactly obsessed by weather, but camping in a tent is certainly more pleasant when the weather is good. We were prepared for the cool days and still colder nights. We were still young then. All we needed was a good sleeping bag, another warm body, and a small electric heater.

Day one, we made it to a campground in Iowa. The day had been warm and the night balmy for that time of year. The new larger tent went up without a problem. We were pros after all. The next morning we were quite pleased to find the canvas dry. Normally, we'd expect to find the surface of the tent moist with dew, but not this morning. So in good spirits, we broke camp and continued west.

Day two took us through the desolate beauty of the Badlands. Our destination for the night was the historic town of Deadwood, South Dakota. Nestled in the Black Hills, the city of Deadwood is located in a valley. During the spring before, there had been a flood in the area. The lingering evidence lay in the deep stream bed that ran beside the road and the washed rock about ten feet up the banks of the creek. But it was back to its' normal level now, so, undaunted, we drove into town.

At that time, Deadwood was a small town with some tourist attractions in "Old Town," including the #10 Saloon where Wild Bill Hickock met his fateful end. And high on a hill, was Mount Moriah Cemetery—final resting place of Calamity Jane and her beloved Wild Bill.

The campground we chose was literally terraced out of the side of a hill, which looked more like a mountain from the road in the valley. Chiseled out of rock, was our guess, since there was no way a tent stake could be driven into the ground. We settled for rocks on the corners. Looking back on it now, I think that's when things began to change.

The winds came up during the night with just a bit of light rain. The sides of the tent began to billow like sails in a gale. Okay, I'll admit we were a little nervous because we knew the toll the floods had taken on the area a few months before. We didn't sleep too well the rest of the night, but the rocks held. By morning, everything was bright and beautiful again.

The next day's drive was picturesque. The road into Yellowstone from Cody, Wyoming follows the North Fork of the Shoshone River. The leaves on the Aspen trees along the river were bright yellow, and the sunlight dancing on the water of the river was spectacular.

Once in Yellowstone we made the rounds of Old Faithful, lakes, and waterfalls within the park. We saw an osprey soar toward the falls in the Yellowstone Canyon. A coyote ran along side the road as we followed the Grand Loop to Old Faithful. Continuing our drive, we saw bison grazing peacefully nearby, as if we didn't exist. The view of an absolutely smooth Yellowstone Lake is an image I'll never forget. Toward dusk, we headed South to a campground in the Grand Tetons, when suddenly three moose were in front of us on the road. They were in no hurry to move, so we just watched each other until they finally lumbered off the road. Late on that cold, clear night in the Grand Tetons, we heard the eerie howls of the coyotes—all night long.

By morning everything crunched. It had dropped to ten degrees during the night. What moisture there was in the air simply froze on everything. We silently thanked whoever had given us the two sleeping bags that zipped together as a wedding gift, and we congratulated ourselves for thinking to bring that little electric heater.

The next few days were pleasant, the nights cold and clear, really cold and clear. Soon, it was time to head back home. We had decided to stop at a few of the attractions we had missed on the way West, the most important of which was Mount Rushmore.

We arrived in Rapid City too late in the day to visit Mount Rushmore, but, much to our delight, we found a campground on a bluff overlooking the city. As the sun set, and the lights from the city grew brighter, it almost seemed as if we were perched above the clouds looking down on the stars. The weather was warm enough that we played cards and listened to the radio late into the evening. In fact, the sky was so clear that we didn't even need to pack up the cards, lantern, etc. on the picnic table outside. We did take the radio inside the tent, however, thinking it would help us drift off to sleep. Thinking of it now, "drift" is a good way to describe what happened that night.

About 3:00 a.m. I awoke to the voice of the DJ talking about the clear night sky and the dry night's forecast. So imagine my surprise when my shoe floated past my pillow. You guessed it, we had a downpour outside. Obviously the DJ didn't have a window near him. Doppler Radar was still part of the future in everyday weather forecasting. By 6:00 a.m., we had salvaged and packed everything we could. The car was loaded. It was still raining. We were soaked, but determined to enjoy our sightseeing. We headed for Mount Rushmore.

The monument was truly impressive, with all those presidents crying in the rain. Well that's how it looked to us. In fact it matched our own sprits at that point. Just then we had a thought. We had seen most of the sights we had planned to see. Maybe we could get ahead of the rain if we got on the road and headed East toward home.

It never happened. The rain stayed with us. It didn't matter that we drove straight through. No stops for the night. (Who wanted to sleep in a wet tent, sleeping bag, and clothes anyway.) You get the picture. And, yes, it rained the entire trip back to Michigan.

To this day, we think that trip is where it all started. Back at home, and always optimistic, we still went camping in that tent. But, over time, you have to face facts. There were just too many nights that started out clear and ended in thunder and lightning.

There was the time at Sleeping Bear Dunes National Park, where the ranger actually came around to campsites late one evening with a Weather Service warning to campers about an approaching storm. He suggested that if we were heading home in the morning anyway, it would be wise to leave immediately or batten down everything we could. Now we've camped a lot, but that was the first time we had heard a ranger give a warning like that. We took one look at each other and said simultaneously, "Time to go."

Packing as quickly as we could, we were on the road in less than half an hour. We had been driving fifteen minutes when the storm slammed the coast. When I say storm, I mean storm. A rain-blinding, trees-bending, limbs-falling, thunder-shaking, lightning-striking-–storm. We drove the whole 150 miles home in that weather. Part of the way, we thought we could see the taillights of what we hoped was a semitrailer in front of us. (We sure couldn't see the road.) Suddenly, the lightning began hitting the power lines and transformers beside the road. It was like the Fourth of July fireworks, without the traditional "oohs" and "aahs." In fact, until then, I didn't think it was possible to hold your breath for twenty miles.

Another particularly memorable tenting trip was to a remote piece of land affectionately known as "The Brown Pond." Out in the middle of nowhere, it was accessible only by an overgrown two-track dirt road. The real attraction was a hill overlooking a beautiful little pond and creek. On occasion, that little creek yielded brook trout. One weekend, we decided to camp at the Brown Pond. Our two young nieces were visiting from Ohio, and we wanted to introduce them to the joys of camping. We splashed in the creek during the day. We had supper around the campfire, sang songs, and made S'mores. The night was mild, and the sky was filled with stars: not a cloud in sight. We checked. A gentle breeze was making all of us a little sleepy. So, we put out the fire and went to bed complimenting ourselves on giving the girls such a great experience.

It must have been midnight when the first crack of thunder made us all sit upright in unison. For some reason, a picture of the Olympic Synchronized Swim Team flashed through my head. Not, for long though. To this day, I'm not sure if it was the screaming of the nieces or the thunder and lightning that gave us the most terror.

To calm them down a little, we told them to count the seconds between lightning flashes and thunder with the old one-one thousand, two-one thousand representing the number of miles to the lightning. That plan went South, however, when they only got as far as "one-one."

So we all sat up the rest of the night, with each flash of lightning showing those terrified little faces and the inevitable screams that followed. That trip was when we learned never to pitch our tent on the top of the hill, no matter how cloudless the night sky looked.

We always camped for a weekend in July with brothers and sisters and their families. This particular area was known for drought in the summer. Unless we brought our tent, that is. Eventually someone would ask if we were going to the annual event, and would cautiously inquire whether we were taking the tent. Soon, no one was even kind. Our tent was the butt of rain jokes. We tried not to take it personally, however, it seemed others were coming to the same conclusion as we were.

Deciding there was a logical explanation, we began our own investigation. We checked the roof of the tent for writing that might say, "Rain Here." We wondered if the tent poles might actually be forming some kind of magnetic field when the tent was up. Were they really aluminum? Was it possible that the coating on the tent to make it rain repellent was in fact attracting the rain? Or worse than that—was it us? We never found a reasonable explanation, but we did come to a conclusion. We had to sell the tent, or camp alone for the rest of our lives.

One sister's neighborhood was having a Block Yard Sale the next week, so we asked if we could sell the tent at her sale.

Her reply was, "Absolutely!" (She was one of the July campers.)

Sale morning dawned bright and beautiful. We began to set up the tent. (It was more impressive when up, and surprisingly, had little mildew.) The minute the tent was fully erected, it started to sprinkle. Nothing major, but it progressed to a steady rain. We tried to avoid the glare from the neighbors. The boos and hissing were a little harder to ignore. It seemed our tent's reputation had spread.

As the rain continued, we watched from the inside of the living room, where we could at least stay dry. About mid-morning a car pulled into the driveway. Mom, Dad, and the kids got out of the car and headed straight for the tent. We put on our raincoats, grabbed our umbrellas, and went out to greet them.

I heard my husband say, "Yeah, we decided it's time to trade up to a camper." And, I heard myself say, "You know since it's raining, and the tent is a little wet, let's just take ten dollars off the price for you."

Well, we had a sale. They didn't even want to let it dry out, which was good considering that might not have happened for a few days. They loaded the tent in the back of their car and backed out the driveway.

We waved from the safety of the living room picture window. Before we knew it, our sister and brother-in-law had their arms around us, and we were all jumping up and down for joy. Funny thing though, by the time that innocent family had turned the corner, the rain stopped, and the sun came out, and the most beautiful rainbow stretched across the sky.

Well, we did trade up to a camper, eventually. We even bought another tent. Although far more cautious now, we went to nylon rather than canvas. (Nylon dries faster, you know.) And, yes, we have had a few water-related adventures since. Though now they are few and far between. But, that's another story.
This story should end here. Maybe it's the guilt. The truth is that every time we hear of a flood or severe thunderstorms somewhere in the country, we wonder if that sweet, little family is on vacation. Or who knows, just maybe they've traded up to a camper and knocked ten dollars off the price of a nice

Poetry

Judith Mabee lives on the shore of Lake Michigan where she is always feathering her nest with new poems, new connections. She has been reading and writing poetry since the first grade and continues to be held and stilled by the white paper and the blue water; the freedom of those open spaces.

Heart

Before the snow melts entirely
it certainly doesn't glisten anymore,
but sits in unwanted heaps,
like old bedding
the dog has been sleeping on.
Now, however, even the dog
is no longer interested.
Brown and sooty, collecting anything,
old snow lacks discrimination.

I know about this,
as I sit at the kitchen table
waiting for the soup to cook--
tomato vegetable
in the blue pot.

It is twilight outside,
and I know the sun
is just now hovering
among the salmon clouds over the horizon,
though it is not rosey in here
with no window to see out of.

Still, I know how it is
out there
with the stumbling things
of this world.

I know, because the heart wants
to cradle it all,
and hold on too long
and not let go: dust
and grief, innocence and ash,
the slow boil
in a full pot,
the sun.

~ Judith Mabee

"Doc," is a retired chiropractor who summers on Mackinac Island and winters in San Antonio, Texas.   A regular contributor to San Antonio's *Sun Poetic Times*, Doc is additionally the author of three chapbooks: *Magic Thing, Changing Shirts on the Road,* and *Shipshape.*   He has also published the *Doc Song Book*.

Geography

In the middle of a long ride
I rode past
Grandpama's old farm.

I did not see
the now of it,
but the then.

I remembered
the man and the woman,
the dog and the bee,
the wheel less car,
the green pears.

I remembered
the woodstove and the outhouse,
the tractor and the rabbits,
the old barn and the fallow fields.

And the creek.
And the smells.

I remembered
my older brother saying,
"I was conceived in the
hayloft of that barn."
That invisible barn.

Voices of Michigan

I remembered the visit when
the old dog was gone.
The Christmas when
the old man was gone.
The Thanksgiving when
there was no one to
visit there,
again.
Ever.

In the middle of a long ride
I rode past
a small boy's memories.

It was a very long ride.
When I got home
they were very
far away.

A boy's heart is
a man's distant country.

~"Doc"

> **Terry Wooten** has taken his performance poetry and writing workshop program to thousands at schools, libraries, conferences and festivals across the country for the past seventeen years. He has published seven chapbooks, and his poetry has been included in numerous magazines and anthologies. Terry is the builder and host-poet of Stone Circle Poetry Gatherings.

Troublemaker

At eighty-two years old
Chuck Shinn
was still on the Michigan State Police
troublemakers list.
It was his Flint unionizing days
in the 1930's,
being a Communist
during the Great Depression.

As the new millennium approached
like an eighty miles per hour parade
of material possessions
headed north
out of the city
for the weekend,
Chuck's stubborn simplicity held true
like a good compass
nobody used anymore.

Everywhere he went
the ghosts of Ben Franklin,
Thomas Jefferson
and Joe Hill
traveled along urging,
"Give 'em heck Chuck!

Give 'em heck!"
Chuck was raised a Mennonite
and never could swear very well.

He spent his teen years hoboing
across Woody Guthrie's vision
of our land,
and worked
in the Civilian Conservation Corps
planting white pines
to repair what the lumber barons did.
The tops of those trees
were his favorite steeple.

At the end of his life
and the twentieth century
Chuck believed in
goodness and honesty
for their own sake,
and made no apologies.

~ Terry Wooten

Aram Kabodian grew up in Rochester, Michigan, and has lived in East Lansing for over fifteen years.   He has taught English and Special Education for nine years.   He has written poetry most of his life.   His wife, Judy, is a musician, and their children are Rachel and Aaron.

Lisa

I used to write her love notes,
often.

> She was a cheerleader, and snow queen,
> > and second chair flute
> > > (played melody...
> > > > happy notes...).

> I was
> > nobody really,
> > > eighth-chair clarinet
> > > > (played background...
> > > > > low, whole notes).

She was kind about it,
seemed to read them.
Wrote back once
or twice:

> short notes of recognition
> > (locks off a goddess, left-overs,
> > > charity).
> I kept them in my pocket
> for weeks.
> They'd get so the ink would blur
> from the sweat
> in the creases of my pants.
> I didn't care. I knew the words

by heart: She called me
"sweet," "a nice guy," "a good friend."

I wonder if she ever told
anyone.
    Was I a secret
        or
    the laughing stock of the girls' locker room
    and the flute section?
       (Don't fool yourself,
        you were a big-time secret...
        embarrassing, curious, weird.)

Last I heard,
she was teaching English in   Minnesota.

I taught English in some of the same
rooms that I gave her notes in
almost   twenty
             years
             earlier.

I hadn't thought of her for years,
and then
I intercepted a note
passing among my seventh graders.
Sealed very well --- taped, stapled:

      "I love you, love you, love you, Lisa.
                --- Jay."

The class wanted me to read it
aloud.

It was as if she walked through
the door and looked me straight
in the eye.

I put it in my pocket.

At the end of the hour,

I gave it to Lisa

       one more time.

~ Aram Kabodian

Gabriela Deckinga was born in La Paz, Bolivia and grew up in Mexico City and Petoskey, Michigan. A graduate of Hope College, she is now doing linguistic research in Central Asia. The poem, *Language Learning,* expresses the challenges in trying to understand, and be understood, in an unfamiliar culture.

Language Learning

Girishyoxdur--No Entrance. I see
no other doors into the vastness
of the nineteenth-century train station.
My arms are tired of carrying the Jack Daniels bag
full of papers, and I need to find a way into the metro.
I move around the stand of fake flowers, around young boys waving
spools of thread in my face, around
the man selling reading glasses,
around the roundness of the building, but the only door
is to a tea house burping out
the smoke and smell of mutton kebabs.
Up the long outdoor stairs, I pass sacks of walnuts,
tumeric and hot peppers, vendors yelling encrypted words.
The people around me understand the code
I would like to know.
        At the top, I stop to bend by two women
selling persimmons, and a question
        stumbles from my mouth.
They recognize it, and point the way down
        the stairway.
I squint in the sun and thank them.

Looking down on the convolution
of scarfed women holding thin lavash bread, men marching
with tiger-print robes slung over their arms, buckets
of sheep liver steaming in the hot September sun, men shouting

out of white, green, and maroon minibuses, tables bulging
with "Easy English" textbooks, Turkish pencil bags, and
Disney comic books in Russian,
I hope to find my way
in the crowd, and in the coded words of the persimmon ladies.

~Gabriela Deckinga

> **Jim Owen** is a vocalist, instrumentalist, conductor, composer, and songwriter who has appeared in venues throughout the U.S., Europe and Japan. Currently, he conducts the Little Traverse Choral Society, and is a voice instructor at Crooked Tree Arts Center in Petoskey, where he resides with his partner, Kristin.

Former

The lights,
dimmed.
The walls,
bared,
leaving only the faded outlines
of former pictures.
The room,
hushed
by the hollow echo
of late words
of former selves.
The house,
emptied of everything
but the clutter
of former emotions
collecting
dust,
stirred by the draft
from the door,
slightly ajar.

- Jim Owen

Voices of Michigan

Jennifer S. Baggerly was born in Coldwater and spent her youth in
Union City. She received her BA degree from Albion College and
is pursuing a Masters in English at Western Michigan University.
She is a member of the Third Coast Writing Project and presently
teaches at Colon Junior/Senior High School.

A *Soul's Images*

I am from . . .

oiled wooden floors, chili in pots, ebony carvings from
Nigeria, the picture of the courthouse when it burned,
coffeepots that perk on the stove, uneven sidewalks
broken by the maple tree roots, and gathering paper thin
snail shells and bouquets of violets from the river bank.

I am from . . .

Coty loose powder, bath-sized bars of Zest, green Excedrin
bottles filled with broken pieces of chalk, elastic button
bracelets, butter rum life-savers, and orange Circus Peanuts
secretly eaten before breakfast while watching cartoons
on Saturday morning.

I am from . . .

a John Deere 4020 that Grandpa and I took down the
lane, deer at dusk eating the new corn, knowing
everyone on Snow Prairie Road, Brach's chocolates
sold by the pound only during winter -- they melt in the
summer -- and scrapbooks filled just for me, with images
from calendars and magazines held in place with Elmer's
School Glue.

I am from . . .

breath that smells like coffee and cigarettes, hard-working
hands that never come clean, drainage ditches, iodine
for cuts, poison ivy, grapevines tangled in the sycamore
limbs, stone piles, electric wire fences to hold the horses.

I am from . . .
>	a green Dodge pickup with a homemade bed of wood
>	because the first rusted away, a brown Buick with a "go
>	to hell" light, oily patches where diesel fuel spilled,
>	and hay lofts where kittens and raccoons were born.

I am from . . .
>	the hole in the barn through which Grandpa drove a
>	tractor, woodchucks that crawled into irrigation pipes
>	and died, a corn picker that grabbed and tore away my
>	grandpa's right hand, popping popcorn on the stove
>	and lifting the lid to shower the kitchen, and mercury
>	lights that illuminate the farm at night.

I am from . . .
>	Images of the past that ground and nourish my soul.

- Jennifer Baggerly

Jennifer Elizabeth Breeding lives in Romulus, Michigan and enjoys writing, cooking, and spending time with her family. Jennifer, twenty-one, has been writing since the age of nine, and hopes to continue well into old age.

Whole

Light plays off the windowpane,
like a deer's eye caught in headlights.
The glowing sun heaves itself over the horizon,
its face red and sweaty.
I watch the disappearing shadows dance over
the wall as my day commences.
For a moment, life, as I know it, is
luxuriously suspended in time, as a red-stained
warmth spreading across my face,
lulling me and allowing the shadows of time to
dance away,
safe in the cradle of a glorious morning set in
a backdrop of fragrant pine, breezes, and fiery luminescence,
making me whole.

~ Jennifer Breeding

Marilyn L. Pietro was born in Flint, Michigan. She is a graduate of Eastern Michigan University and University of Michigan, and taught elementary school in Flint and Utica, Michigan. She married Michael in 1961 and has three sons and four grandchildren. Home is Lake George and Sterling Heights, Michigan. Marilyn has one poem published by the National Library of Poetry as well as on the Internet at www.Poetry.com.

Something Old, Something New

Many years ago,
with needle and thread,
to beautify a pillowcase so,
my grandmother bent her head.
Smooth to the touch in percale and lace,
its quality undenied,
it was meant to soothe each sleepy face,
a source of beauty and pride.
Embroidery was a skill much prized
in the long ago days of old,
for ladies and also children small-sized
on those winter evenings so cold.
In roses and blues and lavender too,
each tiny stitch sewn with love,
more and more lovely as the pattern grew,
sometimes a blue bird or dove.
Then used through the years
for many curly heads.
Through smiles and tears,
it graced our family's beds.
Finally, kept as an heirloom
on a closet shelf,
it waited in the bedroom
for someone like myself.

My friend's daughter makes pillowcase dolls,
my treasure saved in a perfect way.
To my granddaughters, now the past calls
when they see it every day.
How happy my grandmother would be.
It would put a smile on her face
to see two girls upon my knee,
with the doll made of her pillowcase.

~ Marilyn L. Pietro

> **David Whiting** wrote the poem, *Thanksgiv'n Trapper,* while living in
> Fairbanks, Alaska, where he courted his wife Wanda.   She learned of his
> fondness of poetry and encouraged him to write.   Thus was penned
> *Thanksgiv'n Trapper,* inspired by the writing style of Robert W. Service and
> one of Alaska's favorite works, *The Cremation of Sam McGee.*

Thanksgiv'n Trapper

It was Thanksgiv'n time back in '49,
and the trappin' seemed a mite bit slow.
Well I got it in my head to load the sled,
figuring on to Fairbanks I'd go.

So I harnessed the team, and their eyes were agleam,
cuz they knew they were goin' to run.
I packed my skins and some jugs of gin;
of course, I always pack my gun.

Figured it was time to wine and dine
with some good ol' boys I once knew.
With that in mind, I took the time
to load a hind of caribou.

If I'd figured right, we'd run all night,
but them dogs were mighty strong.
By tomorrow night I'd be quite the sight:
all snockered up and singin' a song.

Well, the night got cold and the wind got bold,
and I began to take on a chill.
Then I caught the sight of a fire's light
in a cabin just over the hill.

When I pulled on in I was ashiverin';
then the door it opens wide.
I heard a voice said, "Get in or get out,"
so I reckoned I'd get inside.

Well, my eyes they see'd, but they didn't believe
what they saw on that devilish night.
A half-dead Ma, two kids, and no Pa
huddled up to the fire's light.

Pa'd left one day and was on his way
to gather his beaver pelts.
He fell prey to a Griz that day,
and all they ever found was his belt.

The kids, they say, she was doing okay,
and then a month ago she fell ill.
Woodpile's out and the food was just about,
it's been weeks since they had their fill.

Well, I knew right then I'd have to settle in
and see if I couldn't bail 'em out.
There'd come the day to get back Fairbanks way
so there was no sense in puttin' on a pout.

So I cleared my head, and went out to the shed
and got the axe and chopped some wood.
In no time at all them cabin walls
was warm and feeling good.

I got the meat so the kids could eat,
and then I got them hides.
I laid their Ma down with the furs all around
and wondered what I'd do if she died.

I cut more wood and did what I could,
even shot a moose passing by.
Fourth day came, fifth was the same
and still she hadn't died.

I was noddin' out when there came such a shout;
Lord, I about filled my boots!
She was up in bed, with a gun to my head,
said, "My name's Lou, now talk or I'll shoot."

"Woman," I said, "you was damn near dead,
and this is how I get repaid?
I've been cuttin' wood and doin' all I could,
and you done screwed up my Thanksgiv'n Day."

She looked at her boys, their eyes filled with joy,
and they said what I said was true.
She laid the gun aside, and tears filled her eyes,
and said, "Mister, I'm indebted to you."

"Indebted like hell, I think it's swell--
I can get out of this wretched place."
I loaded the sled and "See ya'," I said;
and I set me a mighty fast pace.

Well the night got cold and the wind got bold,
but I felt strangely warm
as I watched the sight of her firelight
shining brightly thru the storm.

Yeah, Thanksgiv'n time back in '49,
me and Lou talk about it still
as we watch the sight of our firelight
in our cabin just over the hill.
~ David Whiting, 1986

Voices of Michigan

Seth Kay was born in Howell in 1973. He was raised in Frankenmuth and attended the University of Michigan - Flint, where he majored in history. He was published in the University's literary magazine, *Qua*. He now teaches English, History, Creative Writing and Debate at Battle Creek Central High School.

Woodpiles in Retrospect

My young arms never worked as hard as they did
against the silhouette of December trees,
and a low grumble of the diesel,
sounding as hesitant in its duties as I;
slowing, stopping, backing into the drive:
grinding, whirring.

The slide of a bolt, the cry of hinges
bent against their will,
the basement window became the maw
that would swallow the woodpile
one piece at a time.

The basement window pinned into place,
I knew what was to come,
did my best to barricade myself
from my mother's beckoning –
not malicious, but expectant –
expectations I put on,
as any other layer,
against the wintry chill.

My father hated doing this job on his own,
at least I think he did.

So, with a little coaxing,
the promise of a mug of hot chocolate,
I bundled myself in a thick coat, boots,
knit hat and scarf;
a pair of my father's old gloves,
padding worn almost beyond use-
I wanted no others.
On days when the wind bit, rather than blew,
I put on my own gloves,
atop them, my father's.

Then: out the door, down the steps,
around the house to the driveway,
where the rusty truck,
with a groan and a hiss,
raised its bed,
its woody workload rumbling
onto the drive, ten feet from the house.
Ten feet, so little now,
might as well have been a mile.
The truck lurched away,
the unnatural lingering of its exhaust
promising a return in a month.

With an easy swing,
my father split the many logs into many more,
sending wood chips bouncing off the both of us,
and whichever cat had come to watch.
I grabbed the pieces and tossed them –
haphazardly –
through the open basement window,
liking the loud "thud."
My father split faster than I could throw.
The work would take hours.

Voices of Michigan

I wish to say that I was savoring the moment,
and that was why I moved so slowly,
knowing, in the future, the day would come
when I would no longer take up my father's gloves,
go out to work on the earthy scented pile,
watch my father's crushed-felt fedora bob
with each swing of the ax,
the ice collecting on his mustache....

My father's gloves,
worn through,
rest in my closet,
unused for years.

- Seth Kay

Voices of Michigan

Sam King wrote "The Cutter Mackinaw" song in 1994 for the fifty-year United States Coast Guard Mackinaw Reunion, by request of the ship's Chief Executive Officer at the time. The Mackinaw has been a big part of Cheboygan life and history, and it will be a sad day when she is decommissioned.

The Cutter Mackinaw

The sun is rising high, and the air is cold and clear.
There must be five hundred of us standing on the pier.
We're standing on the pier, and we're gazing up in awe
at the vessel we've come to board: The Cutter Mackinaw.

Icebreakers may come and icebreakers may go,
but the greatest of them all, is the one that we all know.
Lined up next to her, the rest seem kind of small.
There's no boat still afloat like the Cutter Mackinaw.

The Great Lakes is her workplace; in Cheboygan she remains.
She's made to break the frozen lakes and free the shipping lanes.
She frees the shipping lanes from Duluth to Saginaw.
Many a freighter's been released by the Cutter Mackinaw.

She was built in Toledo back in 1944.
Commissioned in December, they launched her from the shore.
They launched her from the shore to Great Lakes ports of call,
and they stationed her in our hometown--she's the Cutter Mackinaw.

In '48, off New York State, near the City of Buffalo,
a dozen ships were locked in ice, and the Mackinaw let them go.
The Mackinaw broke them loose. The Mackinaw freed them all.
Captains tipped their hats, after that, to the Cutter Mackinaw.

She's got six main diesel engines and propellers fore and aft:
That puts ten thousand horses deep, inside this sturdy craft.

She's 290 feet long and shaped like a football.
She's tough as nails up to her rails; she's the Cutter Mackinaw.

If she gets stuck in ice, she'll take care of that.
She'll shift her ballast back and forth in ninety seconds flat.
So don't you worry, boys, if she starts to pitch and yaw.
That's just the rock-n-rollin' of the Cutter Mackinaw.

For more than fifty years, the good ship's worked so hard
to break the way and fly the flag of the United States Coast Guard.
The United States Coast Guard: that's who owns her by law,
but we all feel we share a part of the Cutter Mackinaw.

- Sam King

Kim Beach was inspired to write her poem in the weeks following her youngest sister's wedding.   Sensing her mom felt like an abandoned ship, Kim wanted to reassure her of the ***admiral***able job she had done in launching her children into the world.   One of four siblings, Kim is the crew's balladeer.

The Mother Ship

The last ship left the harbor on the fourth night of December,
a starry, cold, clear night that all good sailors will remember.

The fleet of vessels numbered four with ages young to old,
cruising through the seas of life, precious cargo in each hold.

Crafted from the finest wood, with love these boats were made,
great care was given to insure the best of plans were laid.

Each ship was carefully fitted with the best foul-weather gear,
to handle life's shortcomings, without a hint of fear.

A compass on each vessel keeps the boats straight on their courses,
guided by the passion of their kind creator's forces.

An attitude of fun and games is felt on every deck.
We'll dive for buried treasure at the nearest sunken wreck.

A sister ship, a sister ship, a sister and a brother,
the fleet is "ocean ready" through the guidance of the mother.

And sailing through life's oceans, be it calm or stormy night,
we'll navigate the waters with the love from mother's light.

~ Kim Beach

Battle Creek native **Paul Stebleton** graduated from the University of Michigan.   A Hopwood Award winner, his first chapbook, *Bus Station Meditations*, was published in 1992.   Appearing in periodicals from coast to coast, his poems have been published alongside the works of Beat and Post-Beat giants from Bukowski to Ginsberg.

Beautiful Hands

Hunchbacked woman,
how many Valentine's Day cards have
passed through your hands,
gnarled, rooted hands,
placing all carefully
on the shelf at Woolworth's
at four in the afternoon.

~ Paul Stebleton

Voices of Michigan

Voices of Michigan

Glen David Young teaches high school English at Petoskey High School, writes a book review column, "Literate Matters," for the *Petoskey News Review*, and has published a poem in *Voices of Michigan,* Volume II. Glen and his family spend their summers on Mackinac Island.

Scavenger Birds

Giant Canadas and crows again populate
the fields, foraging for what the gulls
could not hold. Their voices fill the backyard
in the shortened hours of receding
natural color. In the fading light of

late October his mother's cancer
has also returned, the scavenger advancing
through her slight frame, renewed
in the lymphs. His voice wells
with worry, as Brewer's blackbirds

darken the bare maples. I think
we should paint her a barn. The walls
bright white, perhaps. The absence
of night coming out of the fall
grass. Barn swallows, their blue

coats, bright breasts in the eaves.
Possibly, too, we could plant a garden,
a winter hope where the carrots
and kale can hunker against the killing
frost, then offer up nourishment at

the first early signs of northern spring.
Ravens, fattened on the ubiquitous carrion,
the fruit of progress, the certainty of death,
circle above now, as the winds come.
His mother's cancer has returned,

as the scavengers prepare for
the coming winter, the killing cold.

- Glen David Young

Peter Olson was born in Denver, but has summered on Mackinac Island since 1990, where he works for Allied EMS-LifeLink. Until May 2000, he directed the English Department at Hillsdale College, and has published academic articles on Euripides, Ezra Pound, Lorca, Mallarme, and Derek Walcott, among others.

Bears in the Woods

Like an old man gripped by a remembered fall,
tentatively testing the ground before him for obstacles,
I walked the old two-track, overgrown by low ferns.
Letting my feet follow the contours, along and across ruts,
I wondered if this was how a newly blind woman would learn
to read: with her hands, fearing, like the old man, no longer able
to trust his vision to avoid a fall, lest her fingers, or his feet
stray too far from the landmarks of the narrative path: learning
how to bring the world in, through a sense of touch, not light.

A brusque snort from within a denser patch of brush,
marked the graceful explosion of a white-tail,
already retreating through dense undergrowth.
Silent, her tiny hooves synchronized through maple and beech
so thick that my clumsy eyes lost her way,
her passage so different from my own.

People used to come to me for help in spotting
the "bears in the woods" that lay ahead of them,
as they started a new project.
Because I thought I could see clearly,
I thought only a little of the metaphor's power,
using words to map my world in the light of reason,
words like boundary stones creating familiar paths,
ultimately obscured by the ferns at my feet.

But how many times have I, unknowingly, been
close enough to touch Makwa, the Anishinabe bear in the woods?
Her "chur-ooof" and the frantic scrabbling of her yearling cubs'

needle-sharp claws, leaping vertically, effortlessly, so high up
in that wavering beech last spring,
announced they were as startled by me in their woods,
as I was to find them in mine.

And I dream that the next time our paths touch, neither of us
might run, but instead feel the grace of each other's passing,
along overlapping palpable arcs of being,
content with feeling again those joules of nervous energy,
racing joyously along our spines,
shivering Makwa's old lesson into new pathways.

~ Peter Olson

Barbara Stinchcombe was born on a farm west of Pellston, Michigan, and attended and graduated from its public school.   After extensive travel, she settled in Chicago and lived there for twenty years with her family.   Inheriting the homestead drew her back home.   One can "come home again" she discovered, but not unchanged.   For she has changed as the Northwoods itself has changed, yet not totally.

John Pesarcyk, Neighbor
B. 1912—D. September 1999, 87 years

John's footsteps did not follow
that road that ran to <u>D</u>etroit—
Mo-town magnet—
drawing farm boys
into the city and assembly lines
where they made the cars
driven in a world
light years away from farms
their parents had settled:
wrapped in the old ways.
Its customs were sewn into the fabric
of their lives and livelihood,
knowing hardness of work done by hand,
and the regularity of all things
bound in Nature and in God.
John remained on the homestead,
a farm boy, then, farmer, grown
into the seasons of the farm.
Anchored by its patterns in Nature
the farm patterned his person,
in the simple ways of life and hard work.
Not for him the summer vacation allotted
to those citied-farm boys
come back to look at the old place—

no longer called home.
Cocky, they drove around
in their shiny new cars,
their pressed pants and sport shirts,
and they marveled over this stick in the mud,
this "hayseed" who had never left home
to see the world, the city lights.
What did he see,
stuck out on the farm?
His blue eyes and wide smile
responded to their jesting,
and, full of innocence,
might have said how he saw the end of the farm,
where it ran along the West-Forty.
They, superior city types,
wondered about him and his vision:
a vision I never comprehended
until I traveled far, far away,
and in returning, I found the very thing
he must have known all along:
How it was that life held in the cycle of seasons
followed a pattern
in the plowing, the planting,
the growing, and the harvesting,
that went full circle
in a knowledge of God
Who had held the seasons of John's
life in His steady hands.

~ Barbara Stinchcombe

> **Andy Slocum** is a pretty-much retired carpenter who writes what he calls
> Carpenter Poetry. Andy has been writing poetry since he was eight years
> old and short stories for the last ten years.

Dezal

Want to know how to feel like a real man?
I can tell ya how.
I found out for myself.
I've gone to all dezals now.

A real man drives what he wants,
and makes his own darn luck,
and a manly man oughta drive a four-wheel drive,
a big 'ol dezal truck.

I love the way they smell
and love that in-jector noise.
A dezal truck separates the man
from all the other boys.

I love that smoke in the cab
that sometimes makes ya choke,
so thick sometimes
civilians think that it's some kinda joke.

Driving a dezal's
just like puttin money in the bank.
I went and joined Farm Bureau
and got me a dezal fuel oil tank.

I got an endless supply of dezal fuel,
and I'm saving real bucks.
I don't have to get in line
like those gasoline-powered trucks.

The tank leaks, and my neighbor says
he doesn't like the smell,
but I don't really give a damn,
and he can go strait to hell.

Some say breathin' dezal fumes makes ya goofy.
Well, I disagree.
Been breathin dezal all my life;
aint nothin' wrong with me.

Some say dezal's spelled with an "s."
Bull, it's spelled with a "z."
Harvy Dezal, with a "z" invented dezals,
and that's good enough for me.

The smell and sound of a dezal
makes ya feel like a real man,
if you're drivin' a regular pickup
or a big old dezal van.

The average age of dezal truck drivers
is seventy-four or seventy-five,
and it's the fumes, and smell of dezal
that keeps these guys alive.

It's guns and God and dezal
that makes America proud and free.
I grew up on dezal fumes,
and you can see nothin's wrong with me.

I swear dezal fumes won't hurt ya.
In fact they keep ya fit.
I am walking proof of that:
Ha, ha, cough, cough, B.S.

~ Andy Slocum

Rick Weiss is a carpenter living in St. Ignace. He spends his free time either on the water boating, diving, or snow skiing.   He has had many Op-Editorials printed in the Detroit Free Press depicting Upper Peninsula life. Married, with two children, Rick credits Jesus first, in all things.

Carpenter's Square

Sawdust thick in the air
takes me back in my mind to childhood,
and to ruffians who, like me,
played tag in bunks of timber

as we cut, hammer, and did fit
lumber together:
Temperature at twenty degrees and rising
with the smell of snow in the air.
Doing the shingle thing,
working it, working it,
feeling the groove.

At break we grab a nailer
spittin' steel like machine guns
in the quick-draw competition.

Carpenters, boys in grown up clothes.

~ Rick Weiss

Harry V. Berg is an educator, poet, and songwriter. Born in
Detroit in 1918, he spent many summers as a young boy on
Grandma Swanson's farm in Manistee. After World War II, Harry
wrote this poem in homage to youthful innocence, and what it meant
to be a boy on the farm.

A Boy on the Farm

I often think of lane and barn,
when I was ten on Grandma's farm---
indifferent cows and playful dogs,
the be-bop of the summer frogs—
strange music to this city ear
accustomed as it is to hear
from daylight's end, to early morn
the airplane and the auto horn.

Milk-bottle caps and paper boats
make battle ships and racing floats,
the things of interest to a boy
freely spending summer joy.
His closest friend…a gurgling brook.
His nose is buried in a book.
You compliment his enterprise,
until you see his sleeping eyes.

So let him dream a year or two.
Once someone did as much for you.
Too soon will come a time when he
must say good-bye to brook and tree
and walk the corridor of years
through joy and grief,

through laughs and tears.
There'll come a time to act like men,
but none to be a boy again.

- Harry V. Berg

> **Lisbeth A. Lutz** is currently an associate professor at Western
> Michigan University in the College of Education. She has won twice
> the Kalamazoo Community Literary awards in the past few years
> and had a poem published in the March 1998 Western Michigan
> University *Encore* Magazine. She has spent twenty-five years worth
> of summers in the north woods of Michigan, the muse of most of her
> writing.

Brief Encounter with Fragility

Wind off the lake--
waves lap at my feet.
An insignificant butterfly is tossed up
fragile, helpless against the elements.
I lower my outstretched hand.
It crawls up my finger
and out of the wind.
It takes its thread of a tongue
and explores the crevices of my palm,
tasting,
hoping to satisfy its basic need of food and shelter,
but in the wrong place.

I stare at its brushed-gold wings,
its thin bronze legs,
its black tips for feet.
It trusts me not to crush it.
I flinch at this enormous responsibility.
The wind picks up.
With its wings tightly held to its body,
it withdraws its tongue,
eyeing me,
wondering
if its trust is misplaced,
and should it take up battle with the wind.

I snap a flower's head
and put it between my fingers,
as if it just grew there.
With its tongue, it tastes the individual petals
meticulously.
The wind continues to rise
making both of our shelters precarious.
Walking in tiny steps
on the sides of my feet
I head toward the cottage,
so as not to unwittingly dislodge it from
its artificial garden.

Reluctantly
the butterfly climbs from my open hand
onto the whorl of a potted geranium.
The wind tosses the petals,
and it,
but it clings
and shifts
and adjusts
to the reality
that is the wind,
and that I am gentle,
but no flower.

~ Lisbeth Lutz

Jacquelyn Sato teaches freshman composition at Grand Rapids Community College. She writes feature articles for *Lamb Light,* a bi-weekly Christian magazine. She also serves as state editor of *Quest*, the quarterly newsletter of the Michigan Counseling Association, to which she contributes articles on the impact of the Internet on society.

Morning Walk, September Saturday

When we walk early
on a September Saturday
collecting the fall,
we're privy to secrets
later concealed.

The critters that hide
from day
are on display.
We watch them play
before buzzing mowers
scare them to
safe havens
where humans don't yell
or dwell.

Squirrels scamper
up and down
innocent sidewalks.
One stops to stare
in terror
at me--
then flees
up a tree
with a flicker
when I click
my fingers.

But we'll treasure forever
the sound of those
wooden bullets
smacking cement.

Squawking jays swear
as we stoop to glean
from night's wet, green silk
handfuls of hardened tears.

~ Jacquelyn Sato

> **John R. Alberts** dwells near Ironton. After having his "work" published in newspapers, journals, Sunday magazines, and having performed his "work" for crowds in large auditoriums, he has discovered that he still needs to brush his teeth, go to work, bathe, wear clean underwear, and as yet cannot walk on water.

Piano Recital

This is, of course, the end for the pianist.
Seated at her loom, fingers ready to weave
melody stroke by stroke on the grand,
its bulk confident on three squat legs,
lid propped, strings taut.
It will give a full airing of every finger stroke.
False note or true, it's no concern of the keys
complacent in their classic ivory and black.

It began with her, as for all we blissful ignorant,
expelled from our last certain comfort,
unsacked and bloody, slapped, wiped,
and too soon fitted with the iron mantle, Culture.

Noted sheaves thrust at us,
bade to approach the Upright wall,
its jet reflecting dark insinuations
slit end to end by a wide and toothy grin.

How nice now to just sit;
not expected to be any more than witnesses.
Asked only to sit and watch.
It's her turn, not, thank God, ours.

Left to her, the interminable practices.
All the repetitions, all the discordances,
each confident rhythmic march of notes
degenerating into a drunken stumble.

The small miracle of a correct passage
savored while struggling through the next,
inevitably more elaborate note clusters
set upon and between the arbitrary lines.

At last, concordance.
An orange; hide ripped, center invaded,
sections parted, pulp engorged, juice slathered,
made whole again by harping key struck strings.

As she calms the trembled keys
our gathered hands applaud
the melody reborn:
certain it was sent to save us.

~ John Alberts

Appendix

The Editor

Editor **Christina Rajala Dembek** extends her gratitude and joy to the patient, diligent, humorous, and courageous writers within these pages.   Working with the writers and publishers of *Voices of Michigan* taught Christina the yin side of writing and publishing (or would it be yang--depends on the day).   The valuable insights she gleaned from this experience have served to heighten her compassion and appreciation for all that writers and publishers as a group have to go through to accomplish their mission. Whatever happens, it is a group effort, and we all must rely and trust one another to speak truth gently and with a willingness to relinquish our opinions.

Christina resides in Petoskey, Michigan with her loving family and friends, from whom she has learned more than she ever learned through formal education. She extends her thanks to her family for the time freely given to her to accomplish this project. With friend and family Christina has traveled to many places, most understood with the heart. She obtained her Master's Degree from The Johns Hopkins University Writing Seminar program and her B.A. from the Creative Writing Program at The University of Arizona.   She has published non-fiction, but spends most of her time writing poetry and prose.   She began writing at puberty in order to stay sane. Christina is currently a member of the Writer's North group in Petoskey, Michigan, and is, as well, a member of Visions of Peace Drum and Dance Company, Journey, and numerous other unnamed groups all endeavoring to serve.

Assistant Editor

Sharon Frost, our Assistant Editor, has lived so many lives that she could not figure out how to write her own biography (it would take too many pages), so I, a friend, will tell you about her. She is the Muse of Petoskey. No kidding. Sharon believes wholeheartedly that art is the foundation of community, and she makes every effort to help art grow in us (her various recipients of musing) and through us in order to fortify the communal soul. *Voices of Michigan,* the writers, publishers and staff have all benefited from her musing. This is, of course, no easy task, trying to pull artists into full bloom, but amazing things happen with the proper amount of care. We should all be so lucky to know someone such as she. Sharon has a deep and abiding love for her family, also, all of whom enlarge the spirit of place with their presence. Her original work began in occupational therapy, massage and esoteric healing. The musing is a natural outpouring from her hands-on work. She is the founding mother (there is a father) of Visions of Peace Drum and Dance Company; the director for the Chalevoix/Emmet county branch of VSA arts of Michigan which assists all those who cannot access art as easily as the rest of us, and something else too great and ineffable to put into words. She may try to nix this bio, but I will get it into print anyhow.

The Artists

Mary Hramiec-Hoffman (cover artist) was always drawing as a child growing up in the beautiful Petoskey and Harbor Springs resort area surrounding Lake Michigan's Little Traverse Bay. Encouraged by her artistically inclined parents, her drawing ability took on a life of its own. She was enrolled in children's art classes at North Central Michigan College and the Crooked Tree Arts Center in Petoskey by the time she was nine.

Mary continued to develop her talent and obtained her degrees in fine art from St. Thomas Aquinas College and Kendall College of Art and Design. After graduating Mary held the position of creative director at an advertising agency.

Beyond the beauty of the Petoskey and Harbor Springs area, Mary's inspirations emanate from the memories, experiences and sights gained from traveling the United States with her parents, four brothers, three sisters and the family dog in one of America's first motor homes her father expertly fashioned out of a GM delivery truck. Mary still lives in the same scenic resort area in which she grew up with her husband and business partner Mark Hoffman who upholds the business end of the company.

Charity has always been an important issue to Mary and Mark. A portion of all proceeds from the sale of the oil scenes of northern Michigan go toward cancer research and charity programs. In recent years they have favored The National Colorectal Cancer Research Alliance founded in 1999 by Katie Couric, Lilly Tartiioff, and the Entertainment Industry Foundation. Donations have a special meaning to Mary and her family, as she has lost several family members to cancer, including her father in 1985.

Mary is known for the delicate sensitivity portrayed in her oil scenes of northern Michigan. They reflect an appreciation of the fauvist and impressionist movements; she creates a pulsating vibrancy on the surface of her canvases. Behind the spontaneous brushwork and loosely applied colors in her paintings there is control that brings the elements into a structured whole. A series that is increasingly gaining a following for Mary is her "Happy" series. These paintings commonly have polka dot skies and whimsical elements in them. Mary paints on location as well as in her home studio in Harbor Springs. To contact Mary call 231-526-1011 or visit her website, **www.hramiechoffman.com**.

Charlene A. Oestman (interior artist) was born and reared in Michigan and began drawing at the age of five. She retained an interest in art throughout her professional years that were dedicated mostly to the criminal justice system. Now retired, she has studied fine arts at Northwestern Michigan College and Central Michigan and pursues her interest in watercolor, pastels, acrylics and oil paintings as well as drawing. Charlene is a member of the Northwestern Michigan Artists and Craftsmen and resides in Traverse City, Michigan.

Robert Roebuck, the graphic designer for the covers of Volume II and III, hails from Talladega, Alabama but now considers Atlanta, Georgia his home where he has lived for over 11 years.

Professionally, Robert has been a graphic designer for all of those 11 years, but he has always been an artist at heart. He won his first coloring contest at the age of five at Woolworth's department store in Talladega. The grand prize for his mastery of color schemes and keeping well with the lines was a $50.00 shopping spree during the Christmas season. Right then and there Robert knew that the world of art and design was calling his name.

Robert graduated from the Art Institute of Atlanta and now works for an international publishing company where he has honed his computer design skills on a Macintosh, his weapon of choice. He also owns his own design company, Visual Chaos. There he designs products including brochures, corporate identifies, CD/menu/book covers, magazine ads and flyers for a wide range of clients. Robert aspires to be among the greats of the advertising world.

Please feel free to contact him at **vcgrr4@visto.com** for any design needs that you may have.

Volume III Contest Judges

William R. McTaggart is the author of four children's books and the owner of the Gramma Books Publishing Company. He attended the University of Michigan, where he earned his law degree in 1950. Following graduation, McTaggart practiced law in Flint and in Boyne City, Michigan until 1990, at which time he decided to pursue writing, his lifelong passion, full-time. He lives near Petoskey, Michigan.

Wini-Rider Young is a former columnist and Fashion Editor for the *Gazette*, Montreal, Quebec, Canada as well as a former feature writer and Women's editor for *The Florida Times-Union*, Jacksonville, Florida. She is currently Editor-at-large and writer for *Water's Edge*, a Florida lifestyle magazine. Wini spent many a summer in her youth at Harbor Springs, Michigan and still retreats there whenever time allows. Wini critiqued our poems for the contest.

Julie Chamberlain Foust has been a fifth grade teacher for the past twenty-two years and currently is a member of the University Liggett School faculty in Grosse Pointe, Michigan. She is a graduate of Michigan State University. She grew up in East Lansing and spent her summers on the shores of Lake Michigan, sailing port-to-port and always enjoying visits to Mackinac Island. She and her architect husband, Tony, and their almost-grown children love exploring the seasonal beauty at their family retreat in Horton Bay on Lake Charlevoix. Julie has always been active in Junior League, working with children at risk and presenting at national conferences related to child advocacy.

Frederic Sibley has been a student of the fine and mantic arts for over thirty years. His photography has been shown at galleries in Colorado and Florida, and he has published his poetry internationally. For almost a decade, he taught English to both native and non-native speakers at Community Colleges in Washington State. After leaving formal teaching, Frederic has become a professional astrologer in the western psychological tradition. Frederic's poetry appears in Volume two of ***Voices of Michigan, an Anthology of Michigan Authors***.

Joy L. Brown, a resident of Clio, Michigan, is currently caring for her parents, one with Parkinson's disease, and one who is trying to cope. Reading is her escape. Some of her favorite authors are Kurt Vonnegut, John Irving, Julian May and Fred Thornburg (an author in Volume two and three.) Joy was a reader of the short stories.

Pam Meier was born in St. Johns, Michigan and has lived in the Grand Rapids area since the age of two. She earned a Bachelor of Arts degree from Albion College, a Master of Music Education degree from Northern Michigan University, and a Master of Management degree from Aquinas College. She is the Vice President/ General Manager at D.C. Martin and Son Scales, Inc. where she has been employed for the past 15 years. Pam has been a Girl Scout leader for the last seven years and enjoys music, horseback riding, and, of course, reading! Pam and her husband, Chip, have three daughters.

Suzanne Davis is a Marketing Coordinator for the largest Real Estate Company in Kentucky and Southern Indiana. She attended Indiana University, enjoys traveling and has spent many summers on Mackinac Island with her family. Her other hobbies include reading, going to movies, playing a darn good game of volleyball, and horseback riding. Suzi was a fiction reader for the contest and currently lives in Louisville, Kentucky with her two dogs, one cat, and new colt, Calamity Surprise!

Patricia Cameron Cortright lives in East Stroudsburg, Pennyslvania where she is a professional tutor in a wide variety of academic subjects at East Stroudsburg University. She was born and reared in Southfield, Michigan. After moving to Pennyslvania, she received a Bachelor Degree in Psychology and Sociology from East Stroudsburg University and later, while living and working in the Washington D.C. area, added a degree in Elementary Education. Tricia is a member of the McNally Cottage family on Mackinac Island.

Gary Cusack, the third of three children, was born into a strong Irish-Catholic family in 1940 and was reared in Lansing, Michigan. Gary attended Catholic schools in the Lansing area but eventually joined the Army at seventeen along with Elvis Presley at Fort Hood. After leaving the Army, Gary spent six years in pursuit of a college degree, but never succeeded, as he persisted in changing his major and his school every few weeks. He has coursework from Michigan State, Lake Superior, Lansing Community College and North Central Michigan College to name just a few of the Michigan schools he attended. In 1967 he went to work on Mackinac Island as a bartender because a good friend told him, "Mackinac Island is a great place to make money, have fun and meet lots of single young ladies." It is on this Island where he did indeed meet and eventually marry Anna Mary Denneny. Together they have reared five daughters and are the proud grandparents of eleven grand children. Gary and Anna Mary live in Petoskey, Michigan.

Nancy Martin was born and reared in Brookfield, Illinois. Her love of reading began at the age of seven when she discovered the public library and the summer reading program. Now the grandmother of eight, she is still reading – children's books (to keep up with the grand kids), biographies, historical novels, other fiction, and history (especially Great Britian). Additionally, she is interested in genealogy, scrapbooking and ephemeron. Nancy considers herself a reader, not a writer; however, while in high school and at Albion College, she was on the newspaper staff and has written several articles for *Miniature Collector and Contemporary Doll* magazines. She and her husband have lived in Grand Rapids, Michigan for forty-two years and honeymooned on Mackinac Island in 1956.

Cathy Kemp lives in Canton, Michigan with her husband Scott and two boys, Kyle and Colin. She is a graduate, with a degree in English, from Indiana University. Cathy enjoys cooking, reading and traveling. Cathy was a reader in the non-fiction genre.

Joan Maril, MSEd, is an Educational Consultant in Austin, Texas. She has developed programs, written curricula, and obtained grants in the education field. Included in her work are the videos "Silence is Golden" and "Basic Steps to School Success." In addition to the professional work, she has been recognized for her endeavors in both prose and poetry. Joan was one of our non-fiction readers.

Ellen Spearel, Army brat, Air Force wife of fifty one years, and volunteer extraordinaire has spent most of her life traveling due to her father's and husband's military duty. Two highlights of her travels were her high school graduation from the Vienna (Austria) Area School System in 1947 and living in Germany twice. Ellen attended the High Museum, School of Art in Atlanta, Georgia until her marriage in 1949. Her various volunteer activities cover school chaperoning, various Air Force wives' activities, and seventeen years with the Mease Hospital Auxiliary in Florida, where she and husband, Don, enjoy a very active retirement. Ellen notes that she began her volunteering career as a fourteen year-old filling out ration cards for the United States Government O.P.A. (Office of Price Administration) during World War II.

Janet Rathke spent the summers 1999 and 2000 in St. Ignace, Michigan, where she and her husband, Richard, managed a seasonal motel. When not working at the motel, Janet managed the time to work at the Island Bookstore on Mackinac Island. Janet has a BS in Home Economics Education and a Master of Arts degree in Guidance and Counseling from Eastern Michigan University. She has worked for the Cooperative Extension Service in Michigan, Wisconsin and Minnesota, and has worked as well at Barnes and Noble Bookstore in Duluth, Minnesota. For as long as she can remember, books and reading have been a part of her life. Janet was a fiction reader for *Voices*.

Sharon Nelson Bown had a wonderful childhood on a farm near Ames, Iowa. She graduated from Drake University and enjoyed a brief career in marketing research for General Mills, Inc.

This career ended when she married Phil Brown, an Air Force officer, and agreed to live and travel all over the United States and Europe. Along the way, Sharon did earn a teaching certificate for a second brief career, but then came two sons who are now grown and away in College. Sharon is currently involved as a volunteer in various activities from investment club to ladies' chorus and she is enjoying her third career as a medical transcriptionist in Beaver Creek, Ohio.

David R. Maril was born and reared in Oklahoma City, Oklahoma attended Grinnell College and did graduate work in political-geography at the University of Oklahoma. From a long line of doctors, professor, artists and writers, David received no such talents and joined the Air Force during the Viet Nam Conflict and retired after 31 great year of service. Now living in Austin, Texas with his first wife, Joan, they are enjoying retirement and life.

Raenette Palmer is an elementary school teacher in Petoskey, Michigan. She has lived in Harbor Springs where her husband, Steve, has been an elementary principal for seven years. She loves the area and is inspired to write her own works of fiction, one of which, **Santa Quits,** was published two years ago. Raenette has been a member of Big Brother/Big Sisters for two years and spends time each week with her little sister, Elizabeth. Besides writing and teaching, Raenette also enjoys the outdoors, board games, cooking and traveling. She is an artist who creates mosaic pieces, handmade paper pictures, collages and embroidered clothing.

The Publishers

MackinacJane's Publishing Company came to be the summer of 1998 when Jane Winston and Mary Jane Barnwell decided to combine two of their unfulfilled desires: conducting a writing contest and publishing a book. They, with the help of endless other folks, stumbled their way through the first volume of *Voices of Michigan, an Anthology of Michigan Authors* and quickly learned the state of Michigan is full of new authors wanting to be published. Now in its third year, MackinacJane's is still helping authors bring their works before the public and realizing how supportive people throughout Michigan are of this statewide writing contest.

Mary Jane Barnwell is no longer with the project, but her hard work and inspiration still remain with Jane and John Winston who have taken over MackinacJane's Publishing Company and the writing contest.

The Winstons call Mackinac Island, Michigan home during the three months of the summer. During the remainder of the year, Jane and John live in Warner Robins, Georgia where Jane is a member of the Fort Valley State University faculty and John devotes much of his time to *Voices of Michigan.*

They enjoy this project and certainly hope those who have entered the contest and those who purchase the book will be as pleased with this collection of short stories, poems and non-fiction pieces as the publishers and the authors are.

Voices of Michigan

Permission was granted by the following authors for publication of their listed work in this third volume of **Voices of Michigan.**

Alberts, John: *Piano Recital*
Baggerly, Kim: *A Soul's Image*
Barton, Gregory C: *The Assassins*
Beach, Kim: *The Mother Ship*
Berg, Harry V: *A Boy on the Farm*
Bernard, Randolph J: *Captain Gordon's Ghost*
Blackmer, Richard: *A Gift of Love at Christmas*
Breeding, Jennifer Elizabeth: *Whole*
Brown, Matthew: *The Helm*
Burkett, Jodi: *Grown Up Grouchies Go Away*
Casey, Julie Kirsten: *True North*
Costa, Linda: *Eternal Love*
Crain, Randol N: *Geography*
Deckinga, Gabriella: *Language Learning*
Deckinga, John: *The Great Leap*
Diamond-Young, Elena: *Torn From My Heart, A True Story*
Hauge, Chris: *Boundaries, Lance's Story*
Kabodian, Aram: *Lisa*
Kay, Seth J: *Wood Piles in Retrospect*
King, Sam: *The Cutter Mackinaw*
Lambert, Timothy: *The Whine Bottle*
Leslie, Roger: *In The Secret Hearts of Women*
Lutz, Lisbeth: *Brief Encounter with Fragility*
Mabee, Judith: *Heart*
MacDonald, C. Kay: *The Red Hat*
Malmberg, Theresa: *The Forgotten Highway*
Meier, Emily: *Stallion Wannabes*
Moody, Lynn: *As Far As She Could Go*
Olson, Peter: *Bears in the Woods*
Owen, Jim: *Former*
Pietro, Marilyn: *Something Old, Something New*
Radel, Sheri: *The Rain Tent*
Rupe, Mary: *One of God's Fishermen*
Sanecki, Helen: *The Old Jennings Place*
Sato, Jacquelyn Q: *Morning Walk, September Saturday*

Schmeichel, Joan: *Kisses for Laura*
Scott, Mary Lee: *Brotherly Love*
Sibley, Frederic: *The Pleasure of Their Company*
Slocum, Andy: *Dezal*
Starbuck, Veronica Anne: *Everfaithful*
Stebleton, Paul: *Beautiful Hands*
Stegehuis, Dave: *The Eagle*
Stinchcombe, Barbara: *John Pesarcyk, Neighbor*
Thornburg, Fred: *Loathe They Neighbor*
VanBuren, Mike: *Twilight Limited*
Weiss, Richard: *Carpenter's Square*
Whiting, David: *Thanksgiv'n Trapper*
Wooten, Terry: *Troublemaker*
Young, Glen David: *Scavenger Birds*
Zamjohn, Martin Carl: *Depression Ice*

Voices of Michigan, Order Blank:

ISBN 0-9667363-03 – Vol I
ISBN 0-9667363-11 – Vol II
ISBN 0-9667363-38 – Vol III

*Fax orders: 1 (478) 953-5995
*Telephone orders: 1 (478) 953-5995
*Email Orders: macjanes@juno.com
*Postal Orders:
      MackinacJane's Publishing Company
      Voices of Michigan
      PO Box 475
      Mackinac Island, Michigan 49757

Pricing:
*Vol I and II $15.95 plus S&H
*Vol III $18.95 plus S&H
*Michigan sales tax if 6% - no tax when shipping out of Michigan.

Payment:
◊Check
◊Credit card: Master card of VISA
Card number: _____
Name on card: _____
Expiration date: _____
Ship to:
Name: _____
Address: _____
City, State and Zip _____
Phone Number ( ) _____

Voices of Michigan may also be purchased at your local bookstore, or through www.amazon.com / www.barnesandnoble.com / www.voicesofmi.com